Railroad Collectibles, An Illustrated Value Guide

2nd Edition

Stanley L. Baker

COLLECTOR BOOKS

A Division of Schroeder Publishing Co., Inc.

The current values in this book should be used only as a guide. They are not intended to set prices, which vary from one section of the country to another. Auction prices as well as dealer prices vary greatly and are affected by condition as well as demand. Neither the Author nor the Publisher assumes responsibility for any losses that might be incurred as a result of consulting this guide.

The First Edition of this book was published under the title *The Railroadiana Collector's Price Guide.*

Additional copies of this book may be ordered from:

COLLECTOR BOOKS
P.O. Box 3009
Paducah, Kentucky 42001

@ $8.95 Add $1.00 for postage and handling.

Copyright: Stanley Baker, 1981
ISBN: 0-89145-171-4

TABLE OF CONTENTS

INTRODUCTION

The continuing expansion in the buying and selling of railroadiana collectibles, with their value steadily on the increase, has made the compilation of this New Revised Price Guide necessary. Collecting the artifacts from America's railroads has become one of the most popular hobbies in the country today, and collectors and dealers alike need to be aware of the current prices being offered on the many collectibles available in this fast-growing field. Prices have been arrived at by studying the prices realized at antique shows and shops, railroadiana shows and auctions, ads found in the antique trade journals, through the various mail order lists, and among collectors in the field.

A short narrative at the beginning of each listing summarizes the category in as few words as possible, making the Guide easy to use as a handy, take-along reference book. A number of the headings include additional listings relating to that particular category. For example, under Dining Car Collectibles you will find china, glass, silverware, menus, linens and stir sticks. The Lamp section contains the various types used by the railroads down through the years, such as engine classification, tail-end marker, switch-stand, semaphore, inspector's, track-walker's, and the caboose and coach wall lamps. Lanterns (trainmen's) follow in a separate category. Under the headings of Art, Books, Cans, Smoking Accessories, Stationery, Telegraphy and Tickets, multiple listings relating to these categories will be found. Four new categories have been added—Cloth Items, Luggage Stickers, Rolling Stock Relics, and Signs. The miscellaneous section and railroad-related collectibles are listed at the back of the book. To help identify the railroad initials and nicknames used in the guide, you will find a key to the abbreviations following the introduction.

All prices shown are retail, and reflect the current market prices as of this writing. Dealers buying for re-sale pay less, depending upon their mark-up. Prices will often vary from one section of the country to another. Condition plays an important role in pricing. Needless to say, supply and demand is the rule governing all pricing, and sometimes a collector is willing to pay

4

far more than the current market value for an item especially needed to round out his collection. And, of course, there is always the occasional "sleeper" to be found.

As with all antiques, top dollar is paid for rarities, such as an item from an obscure, short-lived or now defunct railroad, or for a choice piece of dining car china, such as the C&O service plate, with its wide gold leaf border and rendition of Gilbert Stuart's Athanaeum portrait of George Washington in the center oval, now realizing over $700.00 as compared to around $300.00 only a few years back. We all realize that there are too many variables for any price to be firm, and the prices listed should be used as a GUIDE and not final authority.

In a price guide such as this, it is of course impossible to list every item that is to be found in every category. My endeavor has been to include a representative listing, so that the reader will be able to get a general idea of the many railroadiana collectibles and their worth. I have tried to be as comprehensive as possible, but new items will always surface, and old ones will continue to be evaluated.

You may ask, "Where is railroadiana to be found?" Railroadiana collectibles are being sold through lists sent out by mail-order dealers, or through the classified ads in various railroad or hobby magazines and general antique publications. Antique shops are good sources, and railroadiana items are showing up more and more at the large antique shows across the country. Occasionally some railroads may hold public sales or auctions of surplus or discontinued items. The retired railroad employee is another source, for many of these men kept their caps and badges, locks and keys, lanterns, ticket punches and so on. If they were not disposed of during the owners' lifetime, the estate sale is often a good source, as are the garage sales, flea markets and auctions. Old secondhand shops are a good place to search. Collectors also do a lot of buying, selling, and trading among themselves. Surplus stocks of switch-stand and other lamps and their accessories are sometimes available from railroad supply companies. Oil cans and other tinware can quite often be obtained from manufacturers in this line. Railroad museums, such as the Baltimore & Ohio Museum in Baltimore, Maryland, sell railroadiana, and the Canadian National Railway publishes a list of railroad items they have for sale. There are other such sources where the collector can obtain railroadiana today.

Railroadiana offers the beginning collector the opportunity to collect historically significant mementos of America's transportation history over the years, and it is still not too late to start your collection. For those with only a limited budget, you will note from the Guide that there are many reasonably priced items to choose from. And for those where space is a problem, you will find that railroadiana collectibles not only include the heavy locomotive bells and switchstand lamps, but keys, locks, buttons, passes, playing cards, and many other smaller items can be picked up, making interesting displays in a limited space. You can choose a single category concentrating for instance on uniform buttons and pins, or china from the dining car, or you can generalize. You may wish to collect a particular railroad, one that perhaps holds a special meaning for you, or pick up memorabilia from as many different railroads as possible. Whatever your preference, the choice is yours.

Needless to say, a thorough study should be made of whatever category you plan to specialize in, in order to acquaint yourself with authentic railroadiana items. Know your subject well before you go out to buy.

Good luck in your search!

KEY TO RAILROAD ABBREVIATIONS

INITIALS	RAILROAD NAME	ALSO KNOWN AS
AA	Ann Arbor RR	
A&GW	Atlantic & Great Western RR	
A&S	Alton & Southern RR	
A ST	Atlanta Street RR	
A&StL	Atlantic & St. Lawrence RR	
AC&S	Atlantic City & Shore RR	
ACL	Atlantic Coat Line RR	
AT&SF	Atchison Topeka & Santa Fe Ry	Santa Fe
B&A	Boston & Albany RR	
B&F	Boston & Fitchburg RR	
B&M	Boston & Maine RR	
B&O	Baltimore & Ohio RR	
BAR	Bangor & Aroostook RR	
BCR&M	Burlington Cedar Rapids & Minnesota RR	
BCR&N	Burlington Cedar Rapids & Northern Ry	
BN	Burlington Northern	
BO&SW	Baltimore Ohio & Southwestern Ry	
BR&P	Buffalo Rochester & Pittsburgh RR	
C&A	Chicago & Alton RR	Alton
C&EI	Chicago & Eastern Illinois RR	
C&G	Columbus & Greenville Ry	
C&NW	Chicago & Northwestern Ry	Northwestern Line
C&O	Chesapeake & Ohio Ry	
C&S	Colorado & Southern Ry	
C&WI	Chicago & Western Indiana RR	
C&WM	Chicago & West Michigan RR	
CB&Q	Chicago Burlington & Quincy RR	Burlington Route

INITIALS	RAILROAD NAME	ALSO KNOWN AS
CC&L	Chicago Cincinnati & Louisville Ry	
CCC	Cape Cod Central RR	
CCC&StL	Cleveland Cincinnati Chicago & St. Louis Ry	Big Four Route
CGW	Chicago Great Western Ry	
CI&L	Chicago Indianapolis & Louisville RR	Monon Route
CM	Colorado Midland	Midland Route
CI&W	Cincinnati Indiana & Western Ry	
CM&PS	Chicago Milwaukee & Puget Sound RR	
CM&StP	Chicago Milwaukee & St. Paul Ry	Milwaukee Road
CMStP&P	Chicago Milwaukee St. Paul & Pacific RR	Milwaukee Road
CNJ	Central RR Co of New Jerssy	
CNR	Canadian National Ry	
CO&G	Chocktaw Oklahoma & Gulf RR	
CPR	Canadian Pacific Ry	
CRI&P	Chicago Rock Island & Pacific RR	Rock Island
CStP&KC	Chicago St. Paul & Kansas City Ry	
CStPM&O	Chicago St. Paul Mpls. & Omaha Ry	Omaha
CV	Central Vermont Ry	
CW&B	Cincinnati Washington & Baltimore RR	
D&H	Delaware & Hudson RR	
D&IR	Duluth & Iron Range RR	
D&RG	Denver & Rio Grande RR	Rio Grande
D&RGW	Denver & Rio Grande Western RR	Rio Grande
D&SF	Denver & Santa Fe Ry	
D&SL	Denver & Salt Lake RR	
DL&W	Delaware Lackawanna & Western RR	Lackawanna

INITIALS   RAILROAD NAME   ALSO KNOWN AS

INITIALS	RAILROAD NAME	ALSO KNOWN AS
DM&IR	Duluth Missabe & Iron Range Ry	
DM&N	Duluth Missabe & Northern Ry	
DM&V	Delaware Maryland & Virginia RR	
DSS&A	Duluth South Shore & Atlantic Ry	
EJ&E	Elgin Joliet & Eastern Ry	
EL	Erie Lackawanna RR	
ERR	Erie RR	Erie
F&NE	Fairchild & Northeastern Ry	
F&PM	Flint & Pere Marquette RR	
FDDM&S	Fort Dodge Des Moines & Southern RR	
FE&MV	Fremont Elkhorn & Missouri Valley RR	
FEC	Florida East Coast RY	
FJ&G	Fonda Johnstown & Gloversville RR	
FRR	Fitchburg RR	
FW&DC	Fort Worth & Denver City Ry	
GB&W	Green Bay & Western RR	
GC&SF	Gulf Colorado & Santa Fe Ry	
GF&A	Gulf Florida & Alabama Ry	
GM&N	Gulf Mobile & Northern RR	
GM&O	Gulf Mobile & Ohio RR	
GN	Great Northern Ry	
GR&P	Grand Rapids & Petoskey Ry	
GTP	Grand Trunk Pacific Ry	
GTR	Grand Trunk Ry System	
GTW	Grand Trunk Western RR	
HBL	Harbor Belt Line RR	
H&BT	Huntingdon & Broad Top RR	
H&NH	Hartford & New Haven RR	
IC	Illinois Central RR	
IHB	Indiana Harbor Belt RR	
IR	Indiana Railroad System	
JC	Jersey Central RR	
K&IT	Kentucky & Indiana Terminal Ry	
KCM&B	Kansas City Memphis & Birmingham RR	

INITIALS   RAILROAD NAME   ALSO KNOWN AS

INITIALS	RAILROAD NAME	ALSO KNOWN AS
KCP&G	Kansas City Pittsburgh & Gulf RR	
KCS	Kansas City Southern Ry	
KCStJ&CB	Kansas City St. Jo. & Council Bluffs RR	
L&N	Louisville & Nashville RR	
L&NE	Lehigh & New England RR	
LI	Long Island RR	
LS&MS	Lake Shore & Michigan Southern Ry	
LV	Lehigh Valley RR	
MEX. NAT.RR	Mexican National RR	
M&I	Minnesota & Internaitonal Ry	
M&NW	Minnesota & Northwestern RR	
M&O	Mobile & Ohio RR	
M&PP	Manitou & Pike's Peak Ry	
M&S	Milwaukee & Superior RR	
M&StL	Minneapolis & St. Louis Ry	
M&StP	Milwaukee & St. Paul Ry	
MC	Michigan Central RR	
MEC	Maine Central RR	
ME	Minneapolis Eastern Ry	
MHC&W	Mississippi Hill City & Western RR	
MKT	Misosuri Kansas Texas RR	Katy
MP	Missouri Pacific RR	Mo-Pac
MRR	Manistee RR	
MN&S	Minneapolis Northfield & Southern Ry	
MS&NI	Michigan Southern & Northern Indiana RR	
MSO	Missabe Southern RR	
MStP&A	Minneapolis St. Paul & Ashland Ry	
MStP&SSM	Mineapolis St. Paul & Sault Ste. Marie Ry	Soo Line
NAT.RYS. MEX.	National Railways of Mexico	

INITIALS	RAILROAD NAME	ALSO KNOWN AS
N&W	Norfolk & Western Ry	
NC	North Carolina RR	
NC&StL	Nashville Chattanooga & St. Louis Ry	
NI	Northern Indiana Ry	
NJC	New Jersey Central	Jersey Central Lines
NKP	New York Chicago & St. Louis RR	Nickel Plate
NP	Northern Pacific Ry	
NWP	Northwestern Pacific RR	
NYB&M	New York Boston & Montreal RR	
NYC	New York Central RR	
NYC&HR	New York Central & Hudson River RR	
NY&NH	New York & New Haven RR	
NYNH&H	New York New Haven & Hartford RR	New Haven
NYC&StL	New York Chicago & St. Louis RR	Nickel Plate
NYLE&W	New York Lake Erie & Western RR	
NYO&W	New York Ontario & Western Ry	
NY&E	New York & Erie RR	
NYP&B	New York Providence & Boston RR	
OR&N	Oregon Railroad & Navigation Co.	
OSL	Oregon Short Line RR	
OVE	Ohio Valley Electric RR	
P&O	Portland & Ogdensburgh RR	
P&PU	Peoria & Pekin Union Ry	
P&R	Philadelphia & Reading Ry	Reading
PC	Penn Central RR	
PE	Pacific Electric Ry	
PM	Pere Marquette RR	
PRR	Pennsylvania RR	Pennsy-Penna
PTRA	Port Terminal Railroad Assn.	
PORT.	Portland RR	

INITIALS   RAILROAD NAME   ALSO KNOWN AS

INITIALS	RAILROAD NAME	ALSO KNOWN AS
PW&B	Philadelphia Wilmington & Baltimore RR	
QA&P	Quanah Acme & Pacific Ry	Quanah Route
REA	Railway Express Agency	
RDG	Reading Ry	
RF&P	Richmond Fredericksburg & Potomac RR	
RI	Rock Island Lines	
RRI&StL	Rockford Rock Island & St. Louis RR	
RUT	Rutland RR	
SAL	Seaboard Air Line Ry	Seaboard
SCL	Seaboard Coast Line RR	Seaboard
SD&A	San Diego & Arizona Ry	
SM	Southern Minnesota RR	
SP	Southern Pacific Co.	
SR	Southern Ry	
SP&S	Spokane Portland & Seattle Ry	
StJ	St. Joe Ry	
StL&SF	St. Louis & San Francisco Ry	Frisco
StL&SW	St. Louis & South Western Ry	Cotton Belt Route
StLIM&S	St. Louis Iron Mountain & Southern Ry	Iron Mountain Route
StL&OR	St. Louis & Ohio River RR	
StP&D	St. Paul & Duluth RR	
StP&P	St. Paul & Pacific RR	
StP&SC	St. Paul & Sioux City RR	
StPCyRy	St. Paul City Railway	
StPM&M	St. Paul Minneapolis & Manitoba Ry	
StPUD	St. Paul Union Depot	
StPUSY	St. Paul Union Stock Yards Co.	
T RY	Toronto Ry	
T&P	Texas & Pacific RR	
TC	Texas Central RR	
TP&W	Toledo Peoria & Western Ry	
TRRA	Terminal Railroad Assn.	
TStL&KC	Toledo St. Louis & Kansas City RR	

INITIALS   RAILROAD NAME   ALSO KNOWN AS

UP	Union Pacific RR	
USTVA	United States Tennessee Valley Authority	
UTC OF IND	United Transit Co. of Indiana	
USY OF O	Union Stock Yards Of Omaha	
V RR	Valley Railroad	
VGN	Virginian Ry	
VL	Vandalia Line	
W&LE	Wheeling & Lake Erie Ry	
W&StP	Winona & St. Peter RR	
WAB	Wabash RR	
W RY	Wheeling Ry	
WC	Wisconsin Central RR	
WM	Western Maryland Ry	
WP	Western Pacific RR	
WP&YR	White Pass & Yukon Route	
WStL&P	Wabash St. Louis & Pacific Ry	
Y&MV	Yazoo & Mississippi Valley RR	

ADVERTISING SOUVENIRS

Thousands of advertising souvenir items, such as paperweights, spoons, fans, letter openers, pocket mirrors, match boxes, and novelty items of all kinds were widely distributed by the railroads down through the years. Earlier pieces are bringing high prices, and those from the later years are priced according to their scarcity and demand. The rare and unique items usually go at auction.

Milwaukee Road grizzly bear

BCR&N: Coin type paperweight, 2¾" dia., "Albert Lea Route" 1890s 50.00

BURLINGTON: Paperweight, First Vista Dome car on base, 1945, silver finish 75.00

BURLINGTON: Stainless steel match case, Zephyrus emblem, 1934 .... 22.50

CANADIAN NATIONAL: Bottle opener, steel, 3¾" long, flat type 5.00

CGW: Round metal paperweight, 2¾", maple leaf emblem on celluloid covering, 1890s........................... 47.50

C&NW: Stainless steel pocket knife, Zippo 10.00

CM&StP: Bronze locomotive clock, "Pioneer Limited," 1890s. (rare) 350.00

CM&StP: Ornate letter opener 5" long, "Chicago & Omaha Short Line" 25.00

CM&StP: Paperweight, electric locomotive 10250 on base, "To Puget Sound Electrified," silver finish 75.00

CM&StP: Grizzly bear paperweight, "Gallatin Gateway to Yellowstone Park," bronze finish 85.00

COTTON BELT ROUTE: Medallion type paperweight, bronze, 3", logo, diesel, lightning bolt, flowers. Reverse side blank 42.50

DM&N: Aluminum collapsible drinking cup, logo and Safety First on cover 7.50

ERIE: Trade card, 1890s. "Time And The Erie Wait For No Man" 8.00

FRISCO SYSTEM: Pocket mirror, train and advertisement on celluloid back 37.50

GN: Safety razor in nickel-plated case, "Compliments of the New Oriental Ltd." 28.00

IC: Jigsaw puzzle, Sioux City Iowa Corn Palace. Box dated 1889 . . . . .60.00

MKT: Cast-iron hinged matchbox, shape of old Katy logo . 65.00

MKT: Pocket diary, Indian Territory, Lady Katy on celluloid covers 37.50

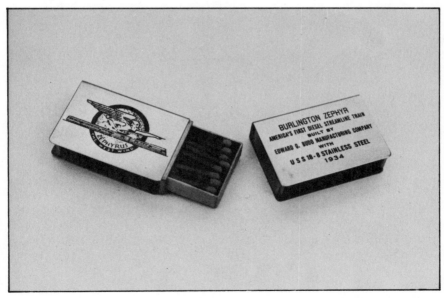

Burlington match case

MP: Round cardboard fan, logo, advertising air-cooled name trains, 1930s 12.50

MP: Bottle opener, metal head, logo, steam engine on pearlized handle 15.00

MP: Pocket knife, Remington, logo steam engine on pearlized handle 22.00

MONON ROUTE: Covered matchbox, alligator shape, bronze. (rare) 200.00

NYC: Paperweight, streamlined locomotive 5445 on base, Britannia metal, silver finish, 1940s 75.00

NYC: Paperweight, locomotive 5200 on base, Britannia metal, silver finish, dated 1928 .... 85.00

Northern Pacific hand fan

NP: Teaspoon, silverplate, "Route Of The Great Big Baked Potato." 27.50

NP: Paperweight, upright bear on cube 4" tall, bronze. The Orme Co 80.00

NP: Baked potato covered inkwell on base, pot metal, decorated 95.00

NP: Miniature bisque bible in original box, "Easter Greetings, 1912," Dining Car Dept 45.00

NP: Bronze letter opener, "Route Of The Great Big Baked Potato" 22.50
NP: Japanese folding fan, logo, ship and train, 1890s 35.00
NP: Green felt pennant, "Route Of The Great Big Baked Potato," 1930s 8.50

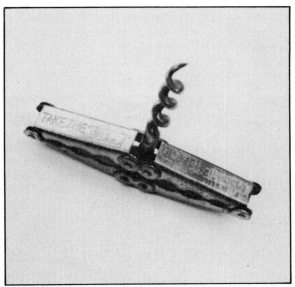

Soo Line cork screw

READING: Memo pad holder, steam locomotive on clip, copper finish, 1920s 55.00
ROCK ISLAND: Glass paperweight, octagon, logo and advertisements, 1880s 85.00
SOO LINE: Tin serving tray, "Montana Success," 1906 . . . . 65.00
SOO LINE: Teaspoon, silverplate, Canadian Rockies in bowl, logo and advertising on handle 22.50
SOO LINE: Folding metal corkscrew, "Take The Soo For Fishing And Hunting" 15.00
SOO LINE: Desk paperweight, magnifying glass center, 1883-1958, Seventy-Fifth Anniversary 28.50
UP: Folding fan, "From Your Fans At Union Pacific Railroad" 5.00
UP: Aluminum token, 1934 Century Of Progress lucky piece 4.50
UP: Aluminum token, 1939 Golden Gate International Exposition 3.50

ADVERTISING WALL POSTERS

The railroads used many colorful posters in the early years to advertise their trains and special travel features, which were posted in conspicuous places to catch the public's eye. Many of these did not survive the years. Value depends on condition, and a rarity will generally bring an exceptionally high price.

Burlington Cedar Rapids
& Northern Harvest poster

Southern Pacific poster

AT&SF—Entitled "Ten Little Navahos," children watching passing train, recent 5.00
BCR&N—Bathing scene at Spirit Lake, Iowa's famous summer resort, Hotel Orleans in background, ca. 1885 . . . . .150.00
BCR&N—Excursion poster promoting harvest excursions to the grain fields of the midwest, ca. 1900 . . . . .50.00
CM—Indian on white horse with CM logo on shield, colorful (rare) 450.00
GN—Photograph of Wm. Crooks and modern locomotive entitled "Yesterday & Today," 1862-1924, free exhibition at GN station, Mpls 35.00
NP—"The Dining Car Route To The Pacific Coast," Minn., N.Dak., Montana, Idaho, Oregon & Washington Territory, ca. 1887 . . . . .130.00
NP—Scenery of Absaroka Mountains, Mont., passenger train in foreground, by Gustav Krollman, ca. 1930s 25.00
PRR—Entitled "Washington The City Beautiful," electric train foreground, capitol and buildings background, ca. 1930s 35.00
SP—Passenger train illustration advertising that Klondikers should take the Shasta Route to Alaska, ca. 1898 . . . . . .100.00
UP—"One Day Saved," The Overland Flyer, large Overland Route UP shield center, ca. 1890 . . . . .125.00
UP—Zion National Park, colorful scene, ca. 1950 . . . . .12.00
UP—Bryce Canyon National Park, Utah, colorful view, ca. 1950 . . . . .12.00
UP—WW II, entitled "In The Service Of Supply" 15.00
UP—WW II, entitled "Giving Them A Helping Hand" 15.00
WAB—Vase of roses, advertising the shortest line to St. Louis, Kansas City, the West and the Southwest, ca. 1886 . . . . . .135.00

Art

Most nineteenth century original railroad art is owned by musuems or is in private collections. Many artists from the early twentieth century produced railroad art that is now being offered for sale at various prices, depending on the fame of the artist. Original Currier & Ives railroad lithographs command very high prices. Other works, such as woodcuts, etchings, engravings, or reproductions of railroad subjects are priced according to their rarity. Old photographs of locomotives and railroad scenes are steadily increasing in value and are now finding their way into collections. Many of these various old pictures hung on the walls

19

of depots and railroad offices. When found intact in their original frames, they usually bring a much higher price.

Original watercolor

Pen and ink drawing

PAINTINGS AND DRAWINGS

Pen and ink drawing, 19½" x 24½", NP Ry's "North Coast
Limited," Helmut Kroening, 1901 . . . . 200.00
Water color, 11" x 20½", NYC & HR RR's "Empire State
Express," Helmut Kroening, 1908 . . . . 350.00
Oil, 11½" x 14½", "Hezekiah Upjohn," railroad tycoon, A.
Sheldon Pennoyer, 1942 . . . . 400.00
Water color, 17¾" x 24½", UP's Fast Mail, "Sherman Hill
'55," Howard Fogg, 1960 . . . . 750.00
Water color, 12¾" x 17½", "Buffalo Hunt Excursion Train,"
Herb Mott, 1961 . . . . 250.00
Pen and ink sketch, 6" x 8", "Old Time Atchison, Topeka &
Santa Fe Train," Herb Mott, 1961 . . . . 75.00
Water color, 13½" x 20½", GN Ry's "Hutchinson Local,"
Pat McMahon, 1962 . . . . 175.00

WOODCUTS, ETCHINGS AND ENGRAVINGS

Woodcut, 7" x 14", "The Village Depot," from *Harper's
Weekly,* 1868. Hand colored 35.00
Etching, 9¼" x 15½", NYNH & H RR Station, Springfield,
Conn. Geo. S. Payne, 1891 . . . . 150.00
Etching, 7¼" x 10¾", "The Last Run," Reynold H.
Weidenaar, 1950 . . . . 55.00

Engraving

Engraving, 7¼" x 10", "Interior Of An American Railway
Car," from *Illustrated London News,* 1861 . . . . .20.00
Engraving, 7¼" x 10¾", "The Depot At Hexham,
Northumberland," England. 1836 . . . . .75.00

BUILDER'S LITHOGRAPHS AND PHOTOGRAPHS

Litho, 22½" x 28¼", CCC RR's "Highland Light," Wm.
Mason, Taunton, Mass., Ch. H. Crosby, Litho, Boston,
ca. 1875, original frame 1000.00
Litho, 16¼" x 26½", 4-4-0 locomotive, The Hinckley
Locomotive Works, Boston, C.H. Crosby & Co. Boston,
ca. 1885, original frame 500.00
Photo, plate 7" x 16", 4-4-0 locomotive, MStP & A, Manchester
Locomotive Works, N.H. Kimball, Photographer, 1890,
original frame 135.00
Photo, plate 8" x 15", 4-8-2 locomotive, Pennsylvania 6800,
Baldwin Locomotive Works, Phila. 1926, framed 50.00

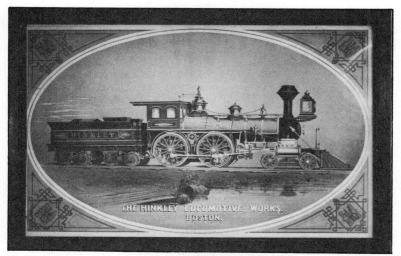

Builder's lithograph

OLD PRINTS AND LITHOGRAPHS

Reproduction, 22" x 24", Missouri Pacific's "Sunshine Special,"
Wm. Harnden Foster, ca. 1920s, original frame 175.00
Calendar print, 18" x 23", "Twentieth Century Limited—
The Greatest Train In The World," Wm. Harnden Foster,
1922, framed 75.00

Calendar print, 16½" x 23", "The World's Greatest Highway,
Horseshoe Curve," Grif Teller, 1934, framed 65.00
Lithograph, 16" x 24¾", "View Of Niagara Falls From
Michigan Central Train," American Lithographic Co.,
N.Y. 1903, original frame 250.00
Lithograph, 18" x 24", "General, The Famous War Engine
Of The Western & Atlantic RR" ca. 1920s, framed 95.00

CURRIER & IVES LITHOGRAPHS

"American Express Train," Palmer del., large folio,
1864 . . . . 3500.00
"American Railroad Scene—Snowbound," small folio,
1871 . . . . 850.00
"The Express Train," J. Schutz del, small folio, N. Currier,
1853 . . . . 575.00
"The Lightning Express Train Leaving The Junction, Palmer
del, large folio, 1863 . . . . 5500.00
"The Railroad Suspension Bridge—near Niagara Falls,
small folio, N. Currier, 1856 . . . . 250.00
"Through To The Pacific, small folio, 1870 . . . . 500.00

Currier & Ives lithograph

OLD PHOTOGRAPHS

Brown monochrome, 16" x 9¼", "Engine Merrimac," Boston,
Lowell & Nashua RR, Mason Machine Co., Taunton,
Mass. 1868 .... 175.00
Photogravure etching, 20¾" x 11½", blue-black, "Empire
State Express," Photogravure & Color Co., New
York, 1906 .... 125.00
Sepia, 8" x 10", CStPM & O's engine No. 157, with
engineer and fireman posing, ca. 1900 .... 50.00
Color, 14" x 21", LS & MS's engine No. 604 pulling
Twentieth Century Limited, Detroit Photographic Co.
1903 .... 150.00
Jackson photo, colored, 15" x 21", passenger train in Rio
Las Animas Canyon, Colo., Detroit Photographic Co.,
1899, original frame 135.00
Colored, 11½" x 12½", Eastern Kentucky mountains along
Louisville & Nashville Railroad's route, ca. 1920,
original frame 45.00
Colored, 8½" x 15½" Chicago & Northwestern's "400"
on stone arch bridge, Minneapolis, ca. 1940s,
original frame 30.00
Colored, 12½" x 25½", Frisco Line's "Firefly" streamlined
steam passenger train, ca. 1930s, original frame 50.00
Colored, 14" x 21", Rock Island's "Rock Island Rocket,"
ca. 1945, original frame 35.00
Colored, 24" x 36", Wabash's streamlined "City Of St. Louis,"
Forest Park, St. Louis, Mo., ca. 1950, original frame 45.00

Old photograph

BAGGAGE AND BRASS CHECKS

Various large rectangular brass checks are found that were used years ago to route travelers' baggage and railroad property pouches. These brass baggage checks came in matched sets on a leather strap. Today the pair are seldom found still intact on the original strap; the duplicate is usually missing, or only a single loose check is found. Many types of small brass tags, mostly round with a single hole in them, can also be found. These were used as time checks, parcel checks, tool checks, key tags, and so on. Many bear the maker's hallmark. Those from remote or obscure railroads are especially desirable and have the higher value.

A ST RR—"A.ST.R.R. #152," 1" x 1 3/8" oval key tag 5.00

B&O—"B.&O.R.R."—1 3/8" diameter "O.R.D. 108" on
   reverse 12.00

B&O—"B.&O.R.R. LOCAL 39590," capitol dome logo,
   rect. 1½" x 2¼" "Am.Ry.Sup.Co.N.Y." 30.00

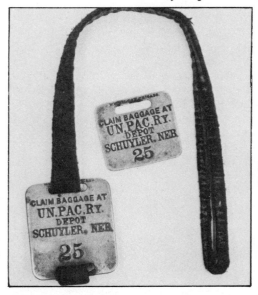

**Baggage checks—
matched pair**

B&OSW—"B.&O.S.W.R.R., Cincinnati, O., Return To General
   Baggage Agent," rect. 2¾" x 2 1/8", strap,
   Am.Ry.S.Co.NY" 35.00

B&M—"BOSTON & MAINE RAILROAD, 58174 WAY,"
   rect. 1 3/8" x 1 3/4", "J. Robbins Mfg. Co. NY" 20.00

Route checks — singles

BCR&N—"Property of The Burlington Cedar Rapids &
Northern Ry. Route, Cedar Rapids, Ia." 2 1/8" x 2½", strap,
"W.W. Wilcox Co., Chgo" 45.00
C&NW—"Property of THE NORTHWESTERN LINE" (logo)
"C.St.P.M.&O.Ry." (below) "St. Paul, Minn." 2½" x 2¼",
strap, "W.W. Wilcox Co., Chgo" 25.00
C&NW—"C.&N.W.RR. 633," time check, 1½" x 1¾", flat
top, round bottom 10.00
CB&Q—"Property of BURLINGTON ROUTE, Chicago,"
2 1/8" x 2½", strap, "W.W. Wilcox Co., Chgo" 22.50
CM&PS—"C.M. & P.S. RY. Milwaukee, Wisc.," 2¼" x 2½",
strap 20.00
CM&StP—"C.M.&St.P.RY. Milwaukee, Wisc.", 2¼" x 2½",
strap 15.00
CRI&P—"CHICAGO R I & PACIFIC RD. 6101," 2½" x 1 3/8",
"Thomas Pat. Feb. 9, 1867" 30.00
GN—"G.N.R.Y. 86," 1¼" diameter, key tag 8.00
GB&W—"G.B. & W.R.R. and K.G.B.&W.R.R. 3527 Local,"
1 5/8" x 2 7/8" "W.W. Wilcox Co. Chgo." 35.00
GT RY—"The Property of GRAND TRUNK RAILWAY
SYSTEM" (logo) "Please return to this Co. as soon as
possible." 2¼" x 3", strap 25.00
ERIE—"EIRE R.R. 416 J.C." 8 sided, 1" across. "Am.Ry.
Sup. Co. N.Y." 10.00
FJ&G—"F.J. &G.R.R. A 649," 1 3/8" dia. "Am.Ry.Sup.Co.
N.Y." 12.50
FJ&G—"Johnstown to Fonda 177 F.J. & G.R.R."—pair on strap,
one large, one smaller duplicate check. "J. Robbins,
Boston." 50.00
H&StJ—"2377 H &St Jo RR," oval tag, 1½" x 1 7/8" 25.00
IC RR—"Return this check to ILL. CENT. R.R. Chicago," old
diamond logo at bottom. 2 1/8" x 2 7/8" "W.W. Wilcox
Co. Chgo." 35.00

Miscellaneous round checks

MC—"The Property Of The MICH.CEN.R.R.CO., Chicago, Ill. Please return to this Co. soon as possible." 1 7/8" x 2¼", strap, "W.W. Wilcox Co. Chgo." 30.00

M&StL—"M. & St. L. Ry. 307 local," 1½" x 1¾", strap ...35.00

NYNH&H—"N.Y.N.H.&H.R.R. 20433 N H," 1 5/8" diameter 15.00

NYNH&H—"Saybrook Junc. and Narragansett Pier 1870, via NYNH&H, NYP&B, and NP RRs." pair on leather strap, one large, one smaller duplicate check. "J.J. Robbins Boston." 65.00

NP—"NORTHERN PACIFIC YELLOWSTONE PARK LINE" (logo) "local," 2¼" x 2½", strap, "Am.Ry.Sup.Co. N.Y." 30.00

OSL RR—"O.S.L.R.R. LOCAL, 01881," 1½" x 2", strap, "W.W. Wilcox, Chgo." 35.00

P&R RY—Time check, "1503 P. & R.RY.CO." 1 3/8" diameter, "Am.Ry.S.Co.Chgo." 12.50

P&R RY—"PHIL. & READ.RY. from ChaddsFord Jct. Pa., Wilmington Br. local X23085," 1½" x 2¼", "Am.Ry.S.Co., N.Y." 30.00

SP—"794 SOU.PAC.R.R. to C.S. & C.C. RY." 1½" x 2", strap 35.00

TC—"2449 TEXAC CENTRAL R.R. LOCAL," 1 5/8" x 2", strap, "Poole Bros., Chgo." 20.00

UP—"Claim baggage at UN.PAC.RY. depot, Schuyler, Neb. 25." pair on leather strap, one large, one smaller duplicate check. "W.W. Wilcox, Chgo." 60.00

WAB—"WABASH R.R. CO. 4," heart shape tag, 1" x 1¼" 8.50

WC RY—"The property of the WISCONSIN CENTRAL RY., Milwaukee, Wisc. LOCAL," 1 7/8" x 2¼", strap, "W.W. Wilcox, Chgo." 25.00

BOOKS

Many books have been written about the railroads since their beginning and up to the present time, covering their history, romance, classic trains, railroad tycoons, and so on. Some bring high prices. Many out-of-print books have increased in value due to their demand. Lucius Beebe's *Mr. Pullman's Elegant Palace Dining Car,* published in 1961 and sold at $17.50, now sells at around $50.00 a copy.

Railroad storybooks from yesteryear—such as the Big Little Books, Horatio Alger, Jr. and Allan Chapman Railroad Series books, and children's colorful railroad picture books, continue to interest the railroadiana collector, and their prices are steadily increasing. The book must be in fine condition, with all the pages intact, to bring a high price.

But most popular of all with collectors is *The Official Guide Of The Railways,* in publication since 1867. Manuals, such as Poor's, Moody's, and others, are also in demand. Textbooks on the locomotive, cars, and railway maintenance are sought after for their pictures and technical data. The earlier copies of these various books in fine condition bring high prices. Various rule books issued by the railroads down through the years are also collectible and priced according to their scarcity.

MANUALS

Bullinger's Postal And Shippers Guide, 1889 . . . . 75.00

Poor's manuals

28

Lyle's Official Railway Manual, 1869-1870 . . . . 130.00
Moody's Steam Railroads Manual, 1925 . . . . 45.00
Moody's Steam Railroads Manual, 1941 . . . . 30.00
Poor's Manual Of The Railroads Of The United States,
    1874-1875 . . . . 125.00
Poor's Manual Of Railroads, 1888 . . . . 115.00
Poor's Manual Of Railroads, 1901 . . . . 85.00
Poor's Railroad And Bankers Manual, 1929 . . . . 65.00

OFFICIAL GUIDES

The Official Guide Of The Railways, March, 1900 . . . . . . 100.00
The Official Guide Of The Railways, June, 1915 . . . . 75.00
The Official Guide Of The Railways, December, 1925 . . . . 65.00
The Official Guide Of The Railways, September, 1935 . . . . 45.00
The Official Guide Of The Railways, October, 1945 . . . . . . 25.00
The Official Guide Of The Railways, October, 1955 . . . . . . 20.00
The Official Guide Of The Railways, October, 1962 . . . . . . 10.00
The Official Guide Of The Railways, June 1969, Golden
    Spike Centennial Issue 8.00

Official guide

29

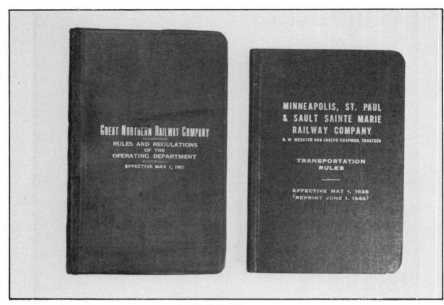

Rule books

RULE BOOKS

AT&SF—*Rules and Regulations*, 1959 ....3.50
CGW—*Book Of Rules*, 1923 ....8.00
C&NW—*Rules for the Government of the Operating
Department*, 1929 ....5.00
C&NW—*Instructions to Ticket Agents & Conductors*, 1881 15.00
CMSt P&P—*Rules & Regulations for Conductors*, 1950 ....4.00
IC—*Rules & Specifications Uniforming of Employees*,
1947 ....6.00
GN—*Book of Rules*, 1908 ....10.00
M&O—*Telegraph Code Book*, 1930 ....15.00
NP—*Rules & Regulations, Operating Department*,
1899 ....12.50
WC—*Rules, Regulations for Telegraphers*, 1903 ......12.00

TEXTBOOKS

Car Builder's Dictionary—Third Thousand, 1881. 491 pages, 84
additional pages of advertisements in back 300.00
Car Builder's Cyclopedia, 13th Edition, 1931, 1260 pages 100.00
Catechism Of The Locomotive—M.N. Forney, 37th Thousand,
1890, 709 pages 22.50

*Hoxsie's Pocket Companion For Locomotive Engineers &
Fireman,* 1875. 104 pages 15.00
Locomotive Catechism—Robert Grimshaw, 13th Edition-
1896, 432 pages 20.00
Locomotive Cyclopedia—10th Edition-1938, 1232
pages 125.00
Railway Engineering And Maintenance Cyclopedia—
4th Edition, 1939, 1008 pages 110.00
Roper's Hand-Book Of The Locomotive, 1874, 324 pages .15.00
Science Of Railways—Marshall M. Kirkman, 1900 (vol. 1
of 12 volumes) 10.00

Text books

RAILROAD BOOKS

Commodore Vanderbilt—Wheaton J. Lane, 1942 ....12.50
Development Of The Locomotive—Central Steel Co.
1925 ....15.00
History Of The Baldwin Locomotive Works,
1831-1923 ....25.00
History Of The Northern Pacific Railroad—Eugene V.
Smalley, 1883 ....65.00
Mr. Pullman's Elegant Palace Car—Lucius Beebe, 1961 ..50.00
Mixed Train Daily—Beebe & Clegg, 1953 (collector's
edition, autographed) 25.00
Railroad Album—John O'Connell, 1954 ....5.00
Railroading From The Head End—S. Kip Farrington, Jr.
1943 ....8.00

31

Railroad books

Romance Of The Rails—Agnes C. Laut, 1929, volumes 1
and 2 ....25.00
Some Classic Trains—Arthur D. Dubin, 1975 ....25.00
Story Of American Railroads—Stewart Holbrook,
1947 ....8.00
Story Of The B&O Railroad, 1827-1927—E. Hungerford,
1928, 2 volumes 25.00
Stories Of The Railroad—John A. Hill, 1899 ....12.50
Wonders And Curiosities Of The Railway—W.S. Kennedy,
1884 ....15.00

WHITMAN BIG LITTLE BOOKS

Chuck Malloy, Railroad Detective, On The Streamliner,
1938 ....6.00
Union Pacific, 1939 ....7.50

BOY'S BOOKS

The Erie Train Boy—Horatio Alger, Jr. 5.00
Ralph And The Missing Mail Pouch—Allen Chapman (1 of
9 Railroad Series 1924) 5.00

CHILDREN'S COLOR RAILROAD PICTURE BOOKS

My Railroad Book—Saml. Gabriel & sons, 1914 ....27.50
On The Railroad—Saafield Co. 1936 ....15.00
Railroad Book—McLoughlin Bros. 1909 ....30.00
Railroad Picture Book—McLoughlin Bros. 1903 ....37.50
The Railway That Glue Built—Fred A. Stokes. 1908 ......35.00

Boy's
books

BREAST BADGES

Breast badges were worn by authorized railroad employees and other personnel connected with the railroads—police, watchmen, dining car stewards, baggage and railway mail service employees, and so on. The badge with the uncommon occupation generally has a higher value. A word of caution: reproduction breast badges are being made.

"C & N W RY POLICE"—six-pointed star, "C & N W POLICE" on raised banner, embossed locomotive in center, number below, nickel plated, 3¼"..........................185.00
"ERIE RAILROAD POLICE"—shield shape, eagle at top, Erie diamond logo at center, black indented letters, nickel plated, 3" high 75.00
"GREAT NORTHERN RAILROAD SPECIAL OFFICER"— shield shape, cut-out star center, black indented letters, nickel plated, 2 3/4" high 125.00

33

Railway police badges

"G. N. RY. SPECIAL POLICE"—six-pointed ball tipped star,
black indented letters, nickel plated, 2 5/8" 95.00

"L.S. & M.S. RAILWAY, D.C.S."—shield shape, black indented
letters, gold plated, 1 3/4" high .60.00

"M. & St.L SPECIAL POLICE"—six-pointed star, black indented
letters, nickel plated, 2 5/8" 100.00

"MISSOURI PACIFIC RR POLICE, SPECIAL AGENT"—
seven-pointed star, enamel inlaid Tennessee State seal at
center, gold finished with floral trim, 2 5/8" 150.00

"N. P. RY. DEPUTY SHERIFF"—six-pointed star, black indented
letters, nickel plated, 2½" 65.00

Railway mail badges

"N. P. RY. WATCHMAN"—six-pointed star, black indented
letters, nickel plated, 2½" 55.00
"N. P. RY. SPECIAL POLICE"—six-pointed star, black indented
letters, nickel plated, 2½" 85.00
"POST OFFICE DEPARTMENT RAILWAY MAIL SERVICE
13415"—embossed designs, oval center with "U.S."
monogram and stars, eagle at top, laurel leaves at bottom,
nickel finish, 2½" high 75.00
"RAILWAY EXPRESS AGENCY POLICE"—six-pointed ball-
tipped star with number in center, black indented letters,
nickel plated, 2 5/8" 65.00
"St. P B & T RY CO. POLICE"—shield shape, cut-out
star center with number, black indented letters, nickel
plated, 2 5/8" 95.00
"ST. P. U. D. 318 BAGGAGE & MAILMAN"—shield shape,
black indented letters, nickel plated, 2 1/8" high 45.00
"S. P. CO. STATION AGENT"—raised on black background,
sheild shape, "STATION" is indented across center,
nickel finish, 2" 50.00
"SOUTHERN PACIFIC RY. CO. SPECIAL POLICE"
w/number—six-pointed star, black indented letters, nickel
plated, 3¼" 85.00

BROTHERHOOD ITEMS

Brotherhood items are a segregated specialty that includes
badges, celluloid pinback buttons, coat lapel buttons and pins,
and other miscellaneous items. Of particular interest are the colorful reversible lodge badges with satin ribbons attached. These
were worn at conventions, funerals and in parades. The coat
lapel buttons issued to members of the Brotherhood for years of
service are also noteworthy; some of these were made of solid
gold. Note: Brotherhood magazines are included in the
magazine section.

BADGES, LODGE — red-white-green gold fringed satin ribbon (backside black,) attached emblem ornaments

"O.R.C.—Div. No. 259, Fond du Lac, Wisc."
9½" x 2¾" 25.00
"B.OF L.F.&E.—Taylor Lodge No. 175, Newark, Ohio,"
9" x 2¾" 30.00

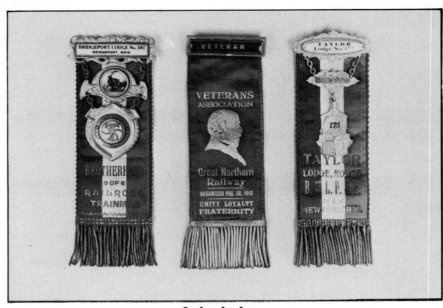

Lodge badges

"B.OF R.R.TRAINMEN—Bridgeport Lodge No. 381, Bridgeport, Ohio," 8½" x 2¾" 30.00
"VETERANS ASSOCIATION, GREAT NORTHERN RY. Memoriam to James J. Hill, Feb. 23, 1913," purple gold fringed satin ribbon 9" x 2¾" 20.00

BADGES, CONVENTION — Pinclasp bar, with or w/o red-white green satin ribbon, attached medal

A.R.S.B.&B.—medal has "Association of Railway Superintendents of Bridges and Buildings," with train, bridge and depot 15.00
B. OF L.E.—medal has "Sixth Triennial Convention, Cleveland, June, 1930," with front view of locomotive 20.00
BROTHERHOOD OF RAILROAD TRAINMEN—Columbus, May, 1909. medal has "9th Biennial Convention," with train, flags across center 32.50
O.R.C.—ticket punch pinclasp bar, medal has "Order of Railroad Conductors," arms emblem, St. Paul, 1901, eagle and wreath 30.00
O.R.C—medal has "38th Session, Mpls. May, 1925," with train on bridge 25.00

Convention badges

LAPEL BUTTONS AND PINS

"B. OF R.R. BRAKEMEN"—gold brakewheel and letters
on black enamel 10.00
"B.R.C.A." (Brotherhood Railway Carmen of America)—
hammer and wrench crossed in center, gold on
black 14.00

Celluloid pinback buttons

"B. OF R.R. CLERKS"—green and red pen and pencil on white background 8.00
"B. OF R.C." (Brotherhood of Railway Clerks)—25 year service pin, red pencil and green quill on white, 10-K ..22.50
"B. OF L.E. HONORARY C.I.D."—2 steam engines in center, 10-K 30.00
"B.L.F. & E."—20 years continuous membership, enamelled red-green-white logo triangle, round pin, 10-K 20.00
"B. OF L.F. & E."—cut-out steam engine, black on gold 12.50
"B. OF R.R.F.H. and B. OF R.C." (Brotherhood of Railway Freight Handlers and Railway Clerks)—dolly & hook, pen & ledger 8.00
"B. OF R.R. TICKET AGENTS"—ticket validator, blue enameled, fancy edge 15.00
"B OF R.T.—BROTHERHOOD RAILROAD TRAINMEN" in red around white, brakewheel with big green T, 15 years, gold wreath around 10.00

Gold coat lapel pin

PINBACK BUTTONS

"B. OF A.R.E.E."—May, 1919, Local 21, baggage car, blue, 1" diameter 8.00
"O.R.C."—Order of Railway Conductors, caboose, 1 1/8" diameter 3.50
"B. OF L.E. OF N.Y.C.S."—Empire State Express, Mch. 20, 1900, 1¾" diameter 27.50

"B. OF L.F. & E."—member, organized 1873, triangle
emblem, 7/8" diameter 5.00
"B. OF R.R. TRAINMEN"—tri-colored BRT monogram, 1"
diameter 4.00
"B. OF R.R. TRAINMEN"—25th Anniversary, 1883-1908,
BT RR emblem, 1¾" 15.00

PAPER & MISC.

B. OF L.F.—Invitation to annual ball, 1888, locomotive
on cover 8.50
B. OF R.R. TRAINMEN—Invitation to annual ball, 1912,
trainman on cover. 5.00
EMBOSSING SEAL—Bro. of Locomotive Engineers,
1889 ....75.00

BUTTONS AND EMBLEM PINS

Uniform buttons have always been popular with the railroadiana collector. These had the name or initials of the railrod stamped on them and came in a gold or silver finish with a flat or domed front. They also were made with the occupation designated on them, such as "Conductor," "Brakeman," "Porter," etc. Most were in the standard coat and sleeve sizes, but other sizes can also be found. Most had a loop back, but they were also made with a patented lock-on back, or, in the case of the cap button, a pronged back. Prices shown are for authentic old buttons in very fine condition. Restrikes are being made today, so carefully study of all buttons is required.

Railroad employees wore various coat lapel emblem pins issued them for years of service, and also wore official insignias on their uniforms. Many of these had enamel inlay work, finely detailed in design, and were either gold finish or real gold. Some collectors specialize in these colorful coat lapel emblem pins.

Railroadmen's work clothing often had brass buttons sewn on them with stamped designs connected with their occupation, as a locomotive, lantern, semaphore, or a railroad-related name. Some of these buttons date back before the turn of the century

Uniform buttons

and few are later than 1930. These work clothing buttons are harder to find than the uniform buttons and bring higher prices.

Uniform buttons

"A C & S RR, SHORE, FAST LINE"—Large, gold, flat 2.50
"A C & S RR, SHORE, FAST LINE"—Small, gold, flat 2.00
"ALTON"—Large, gold, flat 2.50
"ALTON"—Small, gold, flat 2.00
"ANN ARBOR"—Large, gold, flat 3.00
"A & S RY. CO."—Large, gold, flat 3.00
"ATLANTIC & GREAT WESTERN RR"—Large, gold, flat,
    ornate (rare) 25.00
"B & A"—Large, gold, flat 1.75
"B & A"—Small, gold, flat 1.00
"THE B & A"—script, Large, gold, flat 1.75
"THE B & A"—script, Small, gold, flat 1.00
"B & O"—Large, gold, flat 2.25
"BIG FOUR"—Large, silver, flat 4.50
"BOSTON & MAINE R.R."—Maltese cross, Large, silver,
    dome 4.50

Work clothing buttons

"BOSTON & MAINE R.R.". Maltese cross, Small, silver,
dome 3.50
"BURLINGTON ROUTE"—logo, Large, gold, flat 2.00
"CANADIAN NATIONAL RAILWAYS"—crown. Large, gold,
dome 3.50
"CANADIAN NATIONAL RAILWAYS"—crown. Large, silver,
dome 3.00
"CANADIAN PACIFIC"—beaver. Small, silver, dome 2.00
"CANADIAN PACIFIC RAILWAY CO."—monogram. Large,
silver, dome 2.75
"CANADIAN PACIFIC RAILWAY LINES"—shield. Large,
silver, flat 3.00
"C & E I"—Large, gold, flat 1.75
"C & E I"—Small, gold, flat 1.00
"C B & Q"—Large, gold, flat 2.00
"C G W"— ornate script monogram. Large, gold, flat 3.50
"C G W"—ornate script monogram. Small, gold, flat 2.00
"C & I W"—Large, silver, dome 4.00
"CHESAPEAKE & OHIO RAILWAY CO."—Large, silver,
dome 4.00
"C M & St. P."—Large, gold, flat 2.50
"C M & St.P."—Small, gold, flat 1.75
"C M & St.P. RY."—pat. catch. Large, gold, dome 2.50
"C M & St.P. RY."—pat. catch. Small, gold, dome 1.50
"C M St.P & P"—Large, gold, flat .1.50
"C M St.P & P"—Small, gold, flat .1.00
"C & N W"—Large, gold, dome 3.00
"C & N W"—Small, gold, dome 1.75
"C & N W"—Large, silver, dome 2.50
"C & N W"—Small, silver, dome 1.50
"C St.P. M & O"—Large, gold, flat .2.50
"C St.P. M & O"—Prong cap style. Small, gold, dome 3.50
"C. St.P. M & O"—Small, gold, flat 1.10
"C N RR"—Large, silver, flat 1.50
"D & H"—Large, silver, dome 2.00
"D & H"—Small, silver, dome 1.50
"D & H"—The D & H in script, Large, gold, dome 2.25
"D & H"—The D & H in script, Small, gold, dome 1.75
"D M & V"—monogram. Large, gold, dome 6.00
"D & R G W"—monogram. Large, gold, dome 2.50
"D & R G W"—monogram. Small, gold, dome 1.75
"D L & W RR"—Large, gold, dome .3.00
"ERIE"—Large, gold, flat 2.00
"ERIE"—Small, gold, flat 1.75
"FRISCO"—Large, gold, flat 2.50
"G R & P CO."—Large, silver, flat .2.00

"G R & P CO."—Small, silver, flat 1.50
"GRAND TRUNK RR"—around GT monogram. Large,
   silver, dome 3.50
"GRAND TRUNK RR"—around monogram in circle. Large,
   gold, dome 4.00
"GRAND TRUNK RY"—blank circle. Large, silver,
   dome 2.50
"GRAND TRUNK"—Large, gold, dome 1.75
"GREAT NORTHERN RY LINE"—around monogram. Large,
   gold, dome 2.50
"GREAT NORTHERN RY LINE"—around monogram. Small,
gold, dome 2.00
"G M & O"—Large, gold, flat 1.75
"G M & O"—Small, gold, flat 1.00
"H & B T RR"—Large, silver, dome 3.00
"H & B T RR"—Small, silver, dome 2.00
"I C"—Large, silver, flat 2.50
"I C"—Small, silver, flat 1.50
"KANSAS CITY SOUTHERN LINES"—logo. Large, gold,
   flat 1.75
"KATY"—script. Large, gold, flat 1.50
"KATY"—script. Small, gold, flat 1.00
"L V"—Flag logo. Large, gold, flat 2.50
"L V"—Flag logo. Small, gold, flat 2.00
"L&N"—logo. Large, gold, flat 2.50
"L & N"—logo. Small, gold, flat 1.75
"L S & M S RY"—Large, gold, flat 3.50
"L S & M S RY"—Small, gold, flat 2.75
"M & St. L"—script. Large, gold, flat 3.00
"M & St.L"—script. Small, gold, flat 2.25
"M R R"—Large, silver, dome 3.00
"MISSOURI KANSAS & TEXAS"—Large, gold, dome 4.00
"MISSOURI PACIFIC LINES"—Buzz-saw logo. Large, gold,
   flat 1.75
"MISSOURI PACIFIC LINES"—Buzz-saw logo. Large, silver,
   flat 1.50

"MOBILE & OHIO RR"—logo. Large, silver, flat 2.00
"MOBILE & OHIO RR"—logo. Small, silver, flat 1.75
"N C & St.L"—Large, gold, flat 2.50
"N Y C"—Large, gold, flat 1.75
"N Y C"—Small, gold flat 1.25
"N Y C & H RRR"—Large, gold, dome 4.00
"N Y C & St.L. RR CO.—NICKLE PLATE"—Large, silver,
   dome 4.00
"NEW YORK, NEW HAVEN & HARTFORD"—script. Large,
   gold, flat 1.50

"NEW YORK, NEW HAVEN & HARTFORD"—script. Large,
  silver, flat 1.25
"NORTHEASTERN"—logo. Large, gold, flat 2.25
"NORTHEASTERN"—logo. Large, silver, flat 2.00
"NORTHERN INDIANA RAILWAY CO"—Large, gold,
  flat 4.00
"N P"—monogram, pat. catch. Large, gold, dome 1.75
"N P"—monogram, pat. catch. Small, gold, dome 1.00
"N & W"—Large, gold, dome 3.00
"N & W"—Large, silver, dome 2.50
"O V E RY."—Large, silver, dome 3.00
"PENNA."—Large, silver dome 2.50
"P R R"—Large, silver, dome 1.75
"P R R"—Small, silver, dome 1.25
"P R R"—Keystone monogram. Large, silver, dome 1.50
"P R R"—Keystone monogram. Large, gold, dome 1.50

Coat lapel emblem pins

"P C"—monogram. Large, gold, flat 1.00
"PEORIA RAILWAY CO."—Large, gold, flat 3.50
"PERE MARQUETTE"—Large, gold, flat 1.50
"PERE MARQUETTE"—Small, gold, flat 1.00
"P M"—Large, gold, dome 2.00
"P M"—Small, gold, dome 1.75
"PORTLAND RAILROAD"—Large, gold, flat 4.00
"READING LINES"—R in diamond. Large, gold,
  dome 2.50
"ROCK ISLAND LINES"—Star. Large, gold, flat 1.50
"ROCK ISLAND LINES"—Star. Small, gold, flat 1.00
"ROCK ISLAND LINES"—Star. Large, silver, flat 1.50

"ROCK ISLAND LINES"—Star. Small, silver, flat 1.00
"RUTLAND"—Large, silver, dome 2.00
"St. J. RY."—Large, gold, flat 3.50
"SANTA FE"—Large, gold, flat 2.50
"SANTA FE"—Small, gold, flat 1.75
"SEABOARD"—Large, gold, flat 1.50
"SEABOARD"—Large, silver, flat 1.25
"SOO LINE"—patented catch. Large, gold, dome 2.50
"SOO LINE"—patented catch. Small, gold, dome 1.50
"SOUTHERN PACIFIC"—Sunset Lines logo. Large, silver,
dome 10.00
"S P"—monogram. Large, gold, dome 1.50
"S P"—monogram. Small, gold, dome 1.00
"SOUTHERN"—Large, gold, dome 1.50
"SOUTHERN"—Small, silver, dome 1.00
"TORONTO RAILWAY COMPANY"—beaver. Large, gold,
dome 4.00
"UNION PACIFIC"—Large, silver, dome 1.50
"UNION PACIFIC"—Small, silver, dome 1.00
"U T C OF IND."—Large, gold, flat 2.50
"VANDALIA LINE"—VL monogram center. Large, gold,
dome 6.00
"WABASH"—Large, gold, dome 2.50
"WABASH"—pat. catch. Large, silver, dome 2.00
"WESTERN PACIFIC RAILROAD"—Large, gold,
flat 1.50
"WESTERN PACIFIC RAILROAD"—Small, gold, flat 1.00
"YORK ST. RY. CO."—Large, gold, flat 2.50

"ADAMS EXPRESS COMPANY"—Large, gold, flat 8.50
"AMERICAN EXPRESS CO."—Shield, Large, gold,
dome 8.50
"NATIONAL EXPRESS CO."—N inside circle. Large, gold,
dome 8.50
"NEW YORK & BOSTON LINE EXPRESS"—Large, silver,
dome 9.00
"NEW YORK & BOSTON LINE EXPRESS"—Large, gold,
flat 9.00
"PPC CO"—(Pullman Palace Car Co.)—Wreath border,
Large, silver, dome 15.00
"WAGNER PALACE CAR CO."—Winged wheel. Large, gold,
dome 18.00
"AGENT"—Large, gold, dome 4.50
"AGENT"—Small, gold, dome 3.50
"BAGGAGE MASTER"—Large, silver, dome 4.00

"BRAKEMAN"—star. Large, silver, dome 2.00
"BRAKEMAN"—star. Small, silver, dome 1.75
"BRAKEMAN"—wheel. Large, silver, dome 2.50
"BRAKEMAN"—wheel. small, silver, dome 2.00
"BRAKEMAN"—across. Large, silver, flat 1.50
"BRAKEMAN"—across. Small, silver, flat 1.00
"BRAKEMAN—N Y LAKE ERIE & W R R CO"—Large,
    gold, dome, (dual marked) 12.00
"CONDUCTOR"—star. Large, gold, dome 2.00
"CONDUCTOR"—star. Small, gold, dome 1.75
"CONDUCTOR"—across. Large, gold, flat 1.50
"CONDUCTOR"—across. Small, gold, flat 1.00
"CONDUCTOR"—star. St. P & S C RR. Large, gold,
    dome, (dual marked) 12.00
"CONDUCTOR"—beaver. GTR. Large, gold, dome,
    (dual marked) 12.00
"CONDUCTOR"—trolley. St L & OR—Large, gold, dome,
    (dual marked) 12.00
"INSPECTOR"—across. Large, gold, flat 5.00
"MOTORMAN"—star. Large, gold, dome 2.00
"MOTORMAN"—wheel. Small, gold, dome 1.75
"MOTORMAN"—across. Large, silver, dome 1.50
"MOTORMAN"—across. Small, silver, flat 1.00
"PORTER"—star. Large, silver, dome 2.00
"PORTER"—star. Small, silver, dome 1.75
"PORTER"—star. Small, gold, dome 1.75
"PULLMAN"—across. Large, gold, flat 1.75
"PULLMAN"—across. Large, silver, flat 1.75
"PULLMAN"—across. Small, silver, flat 1.00
"PULLMAN"—prong cap style. Small, silver, flat 2.50

COAT LAPEL EMBLEM PINS

ATLANTIC COAST LINE—"Safety Committeeman,"
    white on green 12.00
B & O—Veteran, white capitol dome in blue "V" on
    gold 15.00
BURLINGTON ROUTE—"Safety First" around logo in
    center 15.00
C.M. & St.P. RY.—"Veteran, 25 years," blue on
    gold 12.50
CHICAGO MILWAUKEE ST. PAUL & PACIFIC—
    around Milwaukee Road logo 10.00
C. & N.W. RY. CO.—"Veterans Association" around
    logo 18.00
COTTON BELT ROUTE—logo. Silver and blue 13.00

DULUTH & IRON RANGE RR CO.—"Get The Safety Spirit,"
Indian profile 25.00
GREAT NORTHERN—goat logo, pre-1935 . . . . 17.00
ILLINOIS CENTRAL RAILROAD—around "Safety Always
First" 15.00
LAKE SHORE & MICHIGAN SOUTHERN RY.—mail sack
emblem, 10-K 27.50
MINNEAPOLIS & ST. LOUIS RY. CO.—"The Peoria
Gateway" 22.00
MISSOURI PACIFIC—red buzz-saw logo, "Booster
Club" 10.00
NEW YORK CENTRAL LINES—gold on black, oval 12.00
NORFOLK & WESTERN RY.—"Veteran," steam locomotive,
10-K 25.00
NORTHERN PACIFIC—monad logo, 10-K 20.00
NORTHERN PACIFIC—monad logo, 10-K, "35 years,"
ruby gemstone 45.00
NORTHERN PACIFIC—monad logo, 10-K, "45 years,"
diamond gemstone. 60.00
OMAHA RAILWAY—"Safety veteran—25 years no
injury" 16.00
PENNSYLVANIA RAILROAD—"Veteran," keystone
logo 16.00
UNION PACIFIC—shield logo, "The Overland
Route" 18.00
Y. & M.V. RAILROAD—around "Safety Always
First." 20.00

OFFICIAL LAPEL INSIGNIAS (matched pairs)

"BURLINGTON ROUTE"—rectangular logo 22.00-set
"C M & St. P"—gold cut-out letters 18.00-set
"C & N W"—gold cut-out letters 12.00-set
"KANSAS CITY SOUTHERN LINES"—logo, gold on
red 20.00-set
"THE MILWAUKEE ROAD"—logo, red canted box
logo 20.00-set
THE NORTHWESTERN LINE, F.E. & M.V. R.R."—blue
and black logo (rare) 40.00-set
"OMAHA"—gold cut-out letters 18.00-set
"ROCK ISLAND"—logo, blue letters on gold 16.00-set

RAILROADMEN'S WORK CLOTHES BUTTONS

"CONES BOSS"—embossed lantern, brass 6.00
"FAST LIMITED"—embossed letters, brass 5.00

"MAIL LINE SPECIAL"—embossed locomotive,
brass 9.00
"OSHKOSH BRAND"—embossed locomotive, brass 7.00
"PAYMASTER"—embossed pay car, brass 12.00
"RAILROAD KING"—embossed letters, brass 5.00
"RAILROAD MAN"—embossed profile, brass 8.00
"RAILROAD SIGNAL"—embossed semaphore,
brass 6.00
"ROUNDHOUSE"—embossed roundhouse, brass 12.00
"SWOFFORD'S MOGUL"—embossed locomotive,
brass 6.00
"TEN WHEELER"—embossed locomotive, brass 8.00
"THE ENGINEER"—embossed locomotive, brass 9.00
"THE RAILROAD"—embossed locomotive, brass 8.00
"THE SWITCHMAN"—embossed switch and tracks,
brass 7.50
"UNTITLED"—embossed locomotive, brass 3.50

Lapel insignias

CALENDARS

The railroads gave away many thousands of calendars down through the years, which are now being collected. The rarities are the early color-lithographed calendars from the last quarter of the nineteenth century, which bring very high prices. Of special interest to the collector today are the New York Central and Pennsylvania Railroad's calendars illustrating their famous "name trains" of the steam era. Closely following these are Great Northern's Indian series, done by Winold Reiss in the 1920s and 1930s. There are a great many others with interesting railroad subjects, all very collectible and selling well. Those that have been kept in their original mint condition have the highest value.

AT&SF—1954, Navajo shepherdess, 13¼" x 24¼", all
monthly pages intact 7.50
B&O—1827-1927, Centennial, 20¾" x 28½", painting depicts
laying the first stone, all monthly pages intact 35.00
B&O—1948, large single sheet 21" x 31½", picture has
capitol dome, map, steam and diesel trains, 12 months
printed on bottom half 15.00
BN—1971, large single sheet 26" x 42", photo of diesel train
along Columbia river, 12 months printed on bottom
half 4.00
BURLINGTON ROUTE—1938, 18" x 27", steam engine and
two diesel locomotives, all monthly pages intact 28.00

Chicago Rock Island & Pacific 1888 calendar — unused

Great Northern Indian series — 1928

48

C&O—1948, "Here Comes Your Train, Chessie," 14" x 24", all monthly pages intact 12.50

C&NW—July 1900-June 1901, 8½" x 10½", scenes of picturesque Milwaukee, each page, all monthly pages intact 45.00

C&NW—1937, large Northwestern Line logo, 15" x 23", all monthly pages intact 18.00

C&NW—1941, streamliner 400 on stone arch bridge, 18" x 24", all monthly pages intact 10.00

CRI&P—1888, cardstock sheet 14" x 22", picture of "A. Man" with umbrella with valise, all monthly pages intact 95.00

D&RGW—1944, train in Royal Gorge, Colo., 15" x 25¾", all monthly pages intact 12.50

FEC—1944, map of Florida and freight train, 14" x 24", all montly pages intact 7.50

FRISCO—1962, large single cardstock sheet 22" x 28", top depicts map of system and diesel freight train, 12 months printed below 8.50

New York Central 1926 calendar — mint

GN—May, 1928, one month cardstock sheet, 10¼" x 22", portrait of Chief Two Guns White Calf by Winold Reiss 30.00

GN—June, 1929, one month cardstock sheet, 10¾" x 20½", painting of Many-Clacier Hotel, Lake McDermott, by Adolph Heinze 25.00

GN—February, 1930, one month cardstock sheet, 10" x 22", portrait of Long Time Pipe Woman by Winold Reiss 20.00

GN—1931, complete set 12 months, Indian portraits by
Winold Reiss 150.00
IC—1951, One Hundred Years Of Progress, 1851-1951,
medallion, 18" x 27¼", mint 20.00
M&StL—1945, single sheet 18" x 24½", color photo of steam
locomotive No. 627 pulling freight train, all monthly
pages 35.00
MP—Perpetual tin wall calendar, 12½" x 19", color picture
of new diesel streamliner, the Eagle. All date cards
intact 95.00
NYC—1923, single sheet 25" x 26½", painting "The Greatest
Train In The World"—The 20th Century Ltd. by Wm.
Harnden Foster, mint 50.00
NYC—1926, single sheet 25" x 26½", painting "A National
Institution"—The 20th Century Ltd. by Walter L. Greene,
mint 45.00
NP—1970, single sheet 20½" x 25¾", scene of diesel
freight train emerging from mountain tunnel, 12 months
printed below 4.00
P RR—1935, single sheet 29" x 28½", painting "The World's
Greatest Highway-Horseshoe Curve" by Grif Teller, all
monthly pages intact 45.00
P RR—1947, single sheet, 29" x 28½", painting "Working
Partners" by Grif Teller, all monthly pages
intact 40.00
P RR—1953, single sheet 29" x 28½", painting "Crossroads
Of Commerce," by Grif Teller, all monthly pages
intact 35.00

**Pennsylvania
1947 calendar — mint**

SANTA FE—1929, cardstock panel, 13¾" x 13" "The Blanket"
by E.I. Couse, N.A., all monthly pages gone 15.00
UP—1869-1969 Centennial, 19" x 24" wall type, 8 pages with
16 railroad paintings by Howard Fogg 12.50

CANS, TORCHES & METALWARE

Of the large variety of cans used on the railroads, the most popular with the collector is the engineer's classic long-spout oiler. Next are the various types of kerosene cans. Those from the steam era, marked with the name of the railroad, are much in demand. Those unmarked or with only the manufacturer's name on them have less value. Cans badly dented or rusted must be discounted.

Engineer's long spout oilers

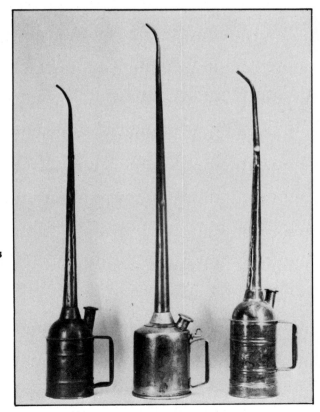

51

Oil burning torches were used in the old days to provide a light while working around the locomotive and in the roundhouse. They were made with a wick, in a variety of styles, shapes, and sizes. A great many were not railroad marked; some were marked only with the name of the manufacturer. Those railroad marked and in fine condition are worth more.

ENGINEER'S LONG SPOUT OILERS

B&O RR—Embossed on front, 30" tall, stop flow lever, "J-Urbana" 25.00
CRI&P RY—Stamped on bottom, 31½" tall, stop flow lever, "Anthes Force" 35.00
DL&W RY—Embossed on side, 29½" tall, stop flow lever, "J—Urbana" 40.00
GN RY—Incised on handle, 30½" tall, stop flow lever, "Eagle" 28.00
NP RY—Embossed on bottom, 30½" tall, stop flow lever, "J-Urbana" 27.50
PRR—Embossed Keystone logo front, 26" tall, no lever, cap only, "J. Urbana" 25.00
SOO RR—Embossed on bottom, 28½" tall, stop flow lever, "Handlan" 30.00

SHORT SPOUT OILER

GN R—Embossed on side tag, 9" spout, pat. Nov. 12, 1912, "Eagle" 20.00
NYC—Stamped around top, 4" spout, "Eagle" 12.00

Long handled torch

KEROSENE OR SIGNAL OIL CANS

AT&SF RY—Embossed near base, ribbed sides, 10½" high,
7" dia. bottom 22.50
CB&Q RR CO. ICC 2A—Stamped on top, ribbed sides, iron
spout, 12" high, 9" diameter bottom. "J-Urbana" 20.00
CStPM&O—Embossed tag rear, 9" high, 6½" diameter base,
"Eagle" 25.00
GN RY—Stamped side of dome, 8½" high, 5¼" diameter
bottom, hand grip, bail, "J-Urbana" 15.00
GN RY—Embossed side of dome, 13" high, 8" diameter bottom,
hand grip, wood spool bail 18.00
NPR—Embossed at side, inverted funnel type, 6" high, 7"
diameter, "J-Urbana" 25.00

Kerosene cans

WATER CANS, GALVANIZED

BURLINGTON ROUTE—Embossed logo on front, 9½" high,
7½" diameter bottom 20.00
CMStP&P RR—Embossed at side, 9¼" high, 7¼" diameter
bottom 12.50

53

DSS&A RR—Embossed side of dome, 12" high, 8" diameter,
lid only 30.00
NYCS—Embossed on side, tea kettle shape, 7" high,
8¼" x 10 7/8" oval bottom 27.50
NP RY—Embossed on side, 14" high, 8½" diameter bottom,
wood spool bail, hinged lid 16.00
SOO LINE—Embossed side of dome, 12" high, 8" diameter
bottom, lid only 15.00

Tallow pots

TORCHES

B&O RR—Embossed on handle, teapot sytle, 4½" high, 5"
handle, "Peter Grey, Boston" 18.50
BURLINGTON ROUTE—Embossed side logo, teapot style, 4¾"
high, 9" handle 25.00
C&NW RY—Bottom marked, cone shaped torch with hook, wick,
9½" tall, "J-Urbana" 25.00
CGW RY—Embossed bottom, coffeepot style, 7" high, 12"
long, bail hook 25.00
CM&StP—Bottom stamped, long spout, teapot type, grip
handle, 6" TALL 20.00
GN RY—Bottom marked, candle type, height 13", all
brass 25.00

M&StL RR—Side embossed, conical type, height 14" 18.50
MO.PAC.RR—Embossed on side plate, long handle torch,
wick, "Eagle" 27.50
SOO LINE—Embossed side logo, teapot style, 4¾" high, 9"
handle 25.00
UP RR—Side marked, cast iron torch, wick, 10" tall,
"Dayton Malleable" 35.00
UNION PACIFIC—Embossed on side plate, long handled
torch, wick, "Eagle" 27.50

TALLOW POTS

C&NW RY—Embossed on bottom, teapot style, 7" high,
5" x 7¼" oval base, "J-Urbana" 15.00
CB&Q RR—Embossed on bottom, teapot style, 7¼" high,
5" x 8" oval base. "Gem" 22.00
GNR—Embossed on side tag, teapot style, 6" high, 5¼" x 7½"
oval base 20.00
M&StLRR—Embossed on side, coffeepot style, side handle,
7½" high, 5" x 8½" oval base 25.00
ROCK ISLAND LINES—Embossed on side, coffeepot style,
7" high, 5" diameter base 18.50
SOO LINE—Embossed on both sides, coffeepot style, 7" high,
5" diameter base 22.50
UNION PACIFIC—Embossed on cap, teapot style, 6" high,
5¼" x 8" oval base 20.00

Funnel

MISCELLANEOUS METALWARE

B&O—Cup, stamped on bottom, 2¾" high, 3½"
diameter 6.00
C&NW RY—Flagman's case, 14½" high, hinged lid, flag
holder, "J-Urbana" 40.00
GN RY—Funnel, embossed, 6" long, 4¼" diameter 10.00
IC RR—Fire bucket, embossed, cone shaped, 13" high,
14½" diameter, red, "Handlan" 35.00
MP LINES—Handled pitcher, embossed, 4" tall, wide
pouring lip 22.00
NPR—Pail, embossed side, 10" high, 12" diameter top 20.00
NPR—Glue pot, stamped side, double boiler type, copper,
7½" high 45.00
StLSF RWY CO.—Water dipper, embossed on bottom,
8" handle 20.00
SOO LINE—Coal scuttle, embossed at rear, 10½"
high 35.00
SOO LINE—Fire bucket, embossed, cone shaped, 19"
high, 13½" diameter red, "J-Urbana" 45.00

Fire bucket

CAP BADGES, CAPS COMPLETE

The cap badge came in a number of styles, from plain rectangular panels to very ornate varieties. Most had black letters against a nickel-plated or gilt background. Others had raised letters and colored enamel work on contrasting backgrounds. Cap badges featuring an unusual occupation or one from an obscure or defunct railroad have a high value. Those not railroad marked, with titles only, such as "Dining Car Steward," "Sleeping, Car Porter," "Conductor" or "Brakeman," are more moderately priced.

Many people collect the cap complete. This includes the badge, cap buttons, and the gold or silver trim cord all intact. Value depends on the cap, badge, and trimmings all being original and having been kept in fine condition down through the years.

"A.T.&S.F. R.R. BRAKEMAN"—nickel finish, plain
rectangle 22.50
"BOSTON & MAINE AGENT"—gold finish, curved
top 20.00
"BOSTON & MAINE BAGGAGE MASTER"—nickel finish,
curved top 35.00
"BOSTON & MAINE CONDUCTOR"—gold finish, curved
top 25.00
"BOSTON & MAINE STATION AGENT"—gold finish,
curved top 22.00
"BOSTON & MAINE TRAINMAN"—nickel finish, curved
top 20.00

**Minnesota
& International
Moosehead
cap badge**

"BUFFALO ROCHESTER AND PITTSBURGH AGENT"—
gold finish, blue logo top 55.00
"BUFFALO ROCHESTER AND PITTSBURGH TRAINMAN"—
silver finish, blue logo top 55.00
"C. & O. RY. CONDUCTOR"—embossed, pebbled
gold background, curved top, milled border 27.50
"C. & O. RY. BRAKEMAN"—embossed, pebbled silver
background, curved top, milled border 25.00
"C.B. & Q. R.R. CONDUCTOR"—nickel finish, plain
rectangle 22.50
"C.G.W. RY. CONDUCTOR"—nickel finish, plain
rectangle 35.00
"C.M. & St. P. AGENT"—embossed, pebbled silver background, fancy pointed top 30.00
C.St.P.M. & O. RY. BRAKEMAN"—nickel finish, plain
rectangle 35.00
C.St.P.M. & O. RY. CONDUCTOR"—nickel finish, plain
rectangle 37.50
"C. & N.W. RY. FREIGHT CONDUCTOR"—nickel finish,
plain rectangle 22.50
C.R.I. & P. BRAKEMAN"—embossed pebbled silver background, curved top 26.00

**Cap with badge
—complete**

C.R.I. & P. CONDUCTOR"—embossed pebbled gold background, curved top 28.00
"D.L. & W. RY. BRAKEMAN"—nickel finish,
plain rectangle 25.00
"G.N. R.R. U.S. MAIL"—nickel finish, fancy pointed
top 45.00

"G.N. RY. BRAKEMAN"—nickel finish, curved top 28.00
"G.N. RY. CONDUCTOR"—nickel finish, curved top 30.00
"GREAT NORTHERN RY. PORTER"—nickel finish, fancy
pointed top 25.00
"GREAT NORTHERN RY. TRAIN SALESMAN"—nickel finish,
fancy pointed top 35.00
"ILLINOIS CENTRAL PORTER"—raised, pebbled silver
background, rectangular 20.00
"L.I. R.R. BRAKEMAN"—nickel finish, plain rectangle . . 20.00
"L.I. R.R. CONDUCTOR"—nickel finish, plain
rectangle 22.00
"L.S. & M.S. FREIGHT CONDUCTOR"—nickel finish, fancy
pointed top 40.00
"MAINE CENTRAL TRAINMAN"—nickel finish, plain
rectangle 20.00
"M.C. R.R. CONDUCTOR"—embossed, pebbled gold back-
ground, "NEW YORK CENTRAL LINES" blue enamel
oval, round top 35.00
"M.C. R.R. OPERATOR"—embossed, pebbled silver back-
ground, "NEW YORK CENTRAL LINES" blue enamel
oval, round top 35.00
"MILWAUKEE ROAD TRAINMAN"—raised, black
rectangular background, logo above 20.00
"MINNESOTA & INTERNATIONAL AGENT"—moosehead in
red and gold logo, top 75.00
"M & St.L RR AGENT"—nickel finish, plain rectangle 55.00
"M & St.L RR CONDUCTOR"—nickel finish, plain
rectangle 55.00
"M & St.L RR CONDUCTOR"—gold on black enamel,
logo at curved top 65.00
"M.St.P. & S.S.M. RY. CO. BAGGAGEMAN"—nickel
finish, plain rectangle 27.50
"M.St.P. & S.S.M. RY. CO. CONDUCTOR"—nickel
finish, plain rectangle 35.00
"M.St.P. & S.S.M. RY. CO. BRAKEMAN"—nickel
finish, plain rectangle 30.00

"NEW YORK CENTRAL CONDUCTOR"—embossed, pebbled
gold background, "NEW YORK CENTRAL LINES" blue
enamel oval, round top 25.00
"N.Y.N.H. & H. RR. BAGGAGE MASTER"—nickel
finish, fancy notched top 28.50
"N.Y.N.H. & H. RR. TRAINMAN"—nickel finish, fancy
notched top 25.00
"N.P. AGENT"—gold on black enamel, "NP" on monad
logo at top 35.00

"NORTHERN PACIFIC RAILWAY BRAKEMAN"—nickel
finish, plain rectangle 22.00
"NORTHERN PACIFIC RAILWAY CONDUCTOR"—nickel
finish, plain rectangle 27.50
"NORTHERN PACIFIC RAILWAY FREIGHT CONDUCTOR"—
nickel finish, plain rectangle 22.00
"P C CONDUCTOR"—red "PC" monogram on gold,
curved top 22.00
"P R R CONDUCTOR"—red Keystone logo, title on pebbled
gold background, ornate top 27.50
"P R R TRAINMAN"—red Keystone logo, title on pebbled
gold background, ornate top 25.00
"P R R USHER"—red Keystone logo, title on pebbled gold
background, ornate top 30.00
"PULLMAN CONDUCTOR"—raised, pebbled gold
background, rectangular 20.00
"PULLMAN PORTER"—raised, pebbled silver
background, rectangular 20.00

Rectangular style cap badges

"ROCK ISLAND BRAKEMAN"—logo in black enamel, raised
title on silver background, arched top 28.00
"ROCK ISLAND CONDUCTOR"—logo in black enamel,
raised title on gold background, arched top 30.00
"SANTA FE BRAKEMAN"—black logo, nickel finish, fancy
pointed top 20.00
"SANTA FE CONDUCTOR"—black logo, nickel finish, high
curved top 25.00

"SOO LINE STATION AGENT"—nickel finish, fancy
pointed top 35.00
"SOUTHERN RY. BRAKEMAN"—nickel finish, curved
top 25.00
"SOUTHERN RY. CONDUCTOR"—nickel finish, curved
top 27.50
"SOUTHERN RY. FLAGMAN"—nickel finish, curved top .30.00
"S. P. CONDUCTOR"—nickel finish, plain rectangle 20.00
"T. St.L. & K.C. R.R. BRAKEMAN"—nickel finish,
curved top 40.00
"UNION PACIFIC BRAKEMAN"—raised, silver pebbled
background, curved top, milled border 35.00
"UNION PACIFIC BRAKEMAN"—silver finish, plain
rectangle 20.00
"UNION PACIFIC R.R. BRAKEMAN"—silver finish, plain
rectangle 20.00
"UNION PACIFIC R.R. CONDUCTOR"—silver finish, plain
rectangle 20.00
"UNION PACIFIC R.R. ELECTRICIAN"—silver finish, plain
rectangle 30.00
"UNION PACIFIC R.R. ELECTRICIAN"—gold finish, plain
rectangle 30.00
"UNION PACIFIC STATION AGENT"—raised, pebbled
gold background, curved top, milled border 35.00
"UNION PACIFIC STATION BAGGAGE"—raised, pebbled
gold background, curved top, milled border 35.00
"UNION PACIFIC R.R. TRUCKMAN"—nickel finish, plain
rectangle 22.50
"WABASH R.R. BRAKEMAN"—nickel finish, fancy notched
top 25.00
"WABASH R.R. CONDUCTOR"—nickel finish, fancy
notched top 30.00

NON-RAILROAD MARKED

"AGENT"—nickel finish, plain rectangle 10.00
"BAGGAGEMAN"—nickel finish, plain rectangle 12.00
"BRAKEMAN"—embossed pebbled silver background, fancy
pointed top 12.00
"CONDUCTOR"—gold finish, plain rectangle 10.00
"DINING CAR STEWARD"—gold finish, curved pointed
top 15.00
"ENGINEER"—nickel finish, plain rectangle 20.00
"FIREMAN"—nickel finish, plain rectangle 20.00
"SLEEPING CAR CONDUCTOR"—gold finish, curved
pointed top 15.00

"SLEEPING CAR PORTER"—silver finish, curved pointed
top 15.00
"TRAINMAN"—nickel finish, plain rectangle 10.00

TRAINMEN'S CAPS COMPLETE WITH BADGE AND TRIMMINGS

"BOSTON & MAINE TRAINMAN"—nickel finish, curved
top badge on deep blue wool cap 35.00
"C.M.St.P. & P. R.R. POLICE OFFICER"—nickel finish,
ornate design, figures, eagle, shield and initials cut-out
on indigo dyed wool cap 85.00
"CONDUCTOR"—on gold braid band around black grosgrain
cap 20.00
"GREAT NORTHERN RY. PORTER"—nickel finish, fancy
pointed top badge on dark blue wool cap 35.00
"GREAT NORTHERN RY. TRAIN SALESMAN"—nickel
finish, fancy pointed top badge on black grosgrain
cap 50.00
"M.C.R.R. NEW YORK CENTRAL LINES CONDUCTOR"—
raised letters on gold pebbled background, blue logo at
top, badge on black grosgrain cap 60.00

Curved and fancy top cap badges

"MILWAUKEE ROAD TRAINMAN"—silver letters on black
enamel, red logo at top, badge on black grosgrain
cap 35.00
"N.P. BRAKEMAN"—silver letters on black enamel, logo at
top, badge on black grosgrain cap 30.00
"PULLMAN CONDUCTOR"—raised black letters on gold
pebbled background, rectangular badge on black
grosgrain cap 30.00
"SOO LINE BRAKEMAN"—raised letters on silver finished
background, blue Soo Line logo in curved top, badge
on black grosgrain cap 50.00
"SOUTHERN RY. CO. FLAGMAN"—nickel finish, curved
top, badge on black grosgrain cap 40.00
"UNION PACIFIC R.R. BRAKEMAN"—rectangular badge on
black grosgrain cap 30.00

CLOTH ITEMS

In addition to the table linens used in dining car service, a variety of other cloth items were in use over the years by the railroads,
most of which are now being collected. This includes towels,
pillow cases, sheets and sleeper blankets, coach car seat cover
headrests, shop cloths or wiping rags, chef's caps, aprons, hot
pad holder, etc. All of these bearing authentic railroad markings on them are being picked up, especially those from roads no
longer in business, which have become scarce and bring the
higher prices. Condition plays an important part in determining
value.

HAND TOWELS

AT&SF—Initials, "AT&SF RY.," 1951, on red center stripe,
white, 13" x 17" 10.00
CMStP&P—Initials, "CMStP&P RR." stamped in black at
bottom, 1956, white, 13½" x 20½" 9.00
GN—"GREAT NORTHERN"on one of two red stripes
forming cross, undated, white, 18" x 24" 15.00
PULLMAN—1914 PULLMAN—PULLMAN 1914" on one of
two blue cross-stripes, white, 16" x 26" 16.00
PULLMAN—"1926 PULLMAN" on blue stripe, white,
17" x 24" 12.00
PULLMAN—"PROPERTY OF THE PULLMAN COMPANY",
1928, blue stripe, white, 17" x 25" 10.50

Headrests

SOO LINE—"19 SOO LINE—SOO LINE 23," on two blue
cross-tripes, white, 16" x 20" 16.00

HEAD RESTS

C&NW—The "400" at bottom, "NORTHWESTERN SYSTEM"
at top, brown on tan, 15" x 19½" 8.00
IC—"ILLINOIS CENTRAL"in script at bottom end, brown
on tan, 15" x 15½" 6.00
IC—Diamond logo at center, slipover double seat type,
egg-shell white, grey logo, 40½" x 14½" 12.00
MILWAUKEE ROAD—red logo, "DOMELINERS" in script,
brown on tan, 13" x 18" 6.00
NP—Monad logo at top, "NORTHERN PACIFIC" at bottom,
black-red-grey on tan, 15" x 18" 5.00
SOUTHERN—Logo at bottom, "LOOK AHEAD—LOOK
SOUTH," green on pink, 15" x 19" 7.50

UP—Winged streamliner motif at bottom, "U.P." at top, red-grey on yellow, 14" x 19" 9.50

SHOP CLOTHS

C&NW—Logo and "STAY ALERT, STAY ALIVE, SAFETY FIRST," repeated, blue on orange, 14" x 17" 4.00
CJ&E RY—Logo and "SAFETY IS YOUR PERSONAL RESPONSIBILITY," repeated, blue on orange, 13½" x 17½" 6.00
IC—Diamond logo, "TAKE CARE, NOT CHANCES, THINK-WORK-LIVE-SAFELY," repeated, blue on white, 18" x 30" 4.00
ROCK ISLAND—Logo, "DON'T GET HURT, LOOK-THINK-BE ALERT," repeated, blue on yellow, 13" x 16" 5.00

PILLOW CASES

BURLINGTON ROUTE—Logo stenciled in black, standard size 3.00

Shop cloths

CMStP&P—Initials stenciled in black, standard size 4.50
PULLMAN—"PULLMAN" stamped near open end, white, standard size 4.00
UP—Shield logo stamped near open end, white, standard size 5.00
UP—"CITY OF SAN FRANCISCO," orange letters in center strip, white, standard size 3.50

SHEETS

UP—Shield logo repeatedly stamped, white,
81" x 64" 10.00
GN RY—repeatedly stamped, white, 81" x 64" 12.00

MISC. CLOTH ITEMS

C&O—Bath towel, "CHESAPEAKE & OHIO RAILWAY"
across center, blue letters on white, 22" x 38" 18.00
"IC—Dish towel, with IC logo and safety slogans in blue,
white 4.00
NP—Hot pad holder, monad logo, "SAFETY AT WORK,
SAFETY AT HOME," red checkered border, 6" x 6" 8.00
PULLMAN—Blanket, rose, with Pullman Co. logo and black
"No. 4" 38.00
SANTA FE—Chefs cap, logo and "DC" stamped in black,
WHITE 12.00

DATE NAILS

Date nails are small nails with the year date raised or indented into the nailhead. Date nails were pounded into the tie when it was laid in the roadbed, remaining visible for research. Those prior to 1910 bear only a single digit, as 6, 7, 8, or two digits, as 02, 05, 07; after that time the last two numbers of the year were shown. Most of these nails come in steel, but copper, aluminum, and even plastic date nails were also made. The heads usually were round, but other shapes can be found. Shanks vary in length. Collecting date nails and classifying them covers a broad field. Some collectors simply try to see how many different types and dates they can find.

The Texas Date Nail Collectors Association, Lufkin, Texas, is a good source to buy, sell, or trade date nails through the mail. Several books have been published on the hobby, available in retail book stores.

A brief listing of date nails is shown here representing railroads in the Minneapolis-St. Paul area.

C&NW—Steel, square head, "7" indented, stubby
1¾" 1.00

66

Tie dating nails

C&NW—Steel, round head, "11" indented, stubby,
  1¾" 5.00
C&NW—Steel, round head, "27" indented 1.00
GN RR—Steel, round head, "07" indented 5.00
GN RR—Steel, round head, "09" indented 3.00
GN RR—Steel, round head, "T7" indented, letter T 5.00
GN RR—Steel, round head, "25" raised 0.50
GN RR—Steel, round head, "31" raised 0.50
IC—Steel, square head, "24" raised 4.00
MILW. ROAD—Steel, round head, "30" raised 0.50

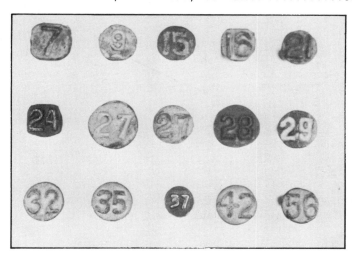

Year dates in the nailhead

MILW. ROAD—Steel, round head, "34" raised 0.50
MILW. ROAD—Copper, round head, "27" indented,
    small 1½" 0.75
MILW. ROAD—Copper, round head, "39" indented,
    small 1½" 0.75
MN&S RY—Steel, round head, "35" raised 0.50
NP—Steel, round head, "11" indented 2.00
NP—Steel, round head, "17" indented 2.00
NP—Steel, square head, "24" raised, square shank 0.75
NP—Steel, round head, "32" raised 0.50
ROCK ISLAND—Steel, round head, "29" raised 0.50
SOO LINE—Steel, round head, "36" raised 0.50

DINING CAR COLLECTIBLES

Dining car collectibles include china, silver, glassware, menus, linens and the miscellaneous stir sticks used in the club car.

Most railroads featured their own exclusive designs on their china, although others used a stock pattern. The railroad's logo, name, or initials appeared on the topside, or they were backstamped, along with the manufacturer's name. There is a great variety of patterns and pieces to be found, the earlier patterns or pieces from short-lived railroads, commanding premium prices. The two popular steam and diesel service plates from the Missouri Pacific, and the Chesapeake &Ohio's famous George Washington plate bring very high prices. All railroad china must be in perfect condition to warrant the prices listed here.

Cups and saucers

Silver holloware consists of the various serving pieces, such as coffeepots, sugar and creamers, cake stands, compotes, bread trays, and the like. They have the railroad's initials or logos on the topside or are railroad-marked on the bottom, along with the maker's name. Many pieces are both top and bottom marked, and these are especially desirable. The earlier pieces were usually quite ornate, while those from the years of the popular "name trains" are more streamlined.

There was a great variety of knives, forks, and spoons used on dining car table settings. These are known as flatware. They, too, came top or bottom-marked or were double marked, and made in a variety of patterns. All silverware must be in perfect condition to have top value. The earlier pieces and those from defunct roads have higher value.

Tumblers, cocktail sets, wine glasses, water pitchers, and other railroad-marked glassware are being collected. The unusual pieces, such as cruets, or cut glass syrup pitchers, are not easily found and are priced high. Most pieces available today are the miscellaneous tumblers and various bar items. Damaged glassware has little or no value.

Dining car menus are much in demand today. Many of them featured very attractive covers, and others were quite ornate. The early menus have a high value. Some menus were in the shape of a special food item the railroad featured in their dining car, as NP's Wenatchee baked apple or famous Idaho baked potato. These unusually shaped menus are especially desirable. Physical condition is an important factor in pricing.

The tablecloths and napkins used on the dining cars of yesteryear are now being collected. These were usually white, although some were colored. Many had the railroad's logo stamped on them, while others had their name or initials woven into the material. Linens showing wear or stains are priced lower.

The miscellaneous stir sticks used in the club car are also now being picked up, along with coasters, paper napkins, toothpicks and such, all railroad marked, of course.

CHINA

China pieces are listed by Railroad, then Pattern Name. More extensive pattern information can be found in Sandknop's dining car china book, *Nothing Could Be Finer.*

China Manufacturers

BSHR:—Bauscher
BUFF:—Buffalo
IRQ:—Iriquois
LAMB:—Lamberton
LEX:—Lenox
LIM:—Limoges
MAD:—Maddock (N.J.)
MDK:—Maddock (Eng.)

MIN:—Minton
MYR:—Mayer
R-D:.Royal Doulton
SCM:—Scammell
SGO:—Shenango
STR:—Sterling
SYR:—Syracuse
WAR:—Warwick

Key to abbreviations:

TM:—Top marked
SM:—Side marked

BM:—Back marked
NBM:—No back mark

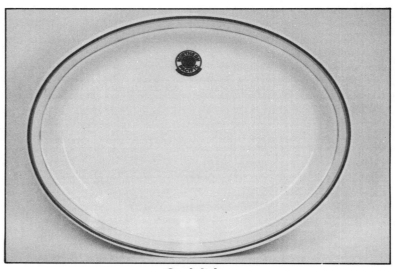

Oval dish

ALASKA—McKinley—5¾" plate, *TM* Mt. McKinley logo,
   NBM, SGO 200.00
AT&SF—Mimbreno—butter pat, flying bird, *BM, SYR* 25.00
AT&SF—California Poppy—cup and suacer, yellow
   poppies, *BM, SYR* 35.00
AT&SF—Griffon—9¾" plate, mythical lion-eagle border
   design, *BM, BSHR* 225.00
AT&SF—Bleeding Blue—12¼" x 5¾" celery, *TM* blue
   Santa Fe, *NBS, SCM* 110.00
ACL—Carolina—9" dinner plate, grey pinstripe border,
   BM, STR 50.00

B&O—Centennial—9" dinner plate, Lord Baltimore
locomotive in border, *BM, SCM* .75.00
B&O—Centennial—10½" dinner plate, diesel-electric #51
locomotive, *BM, LAMB* 45.00
B&O—Centennial—10½" dinner plate, Cincinnatian in
border, *BM, SGO* 12.95
B&O—Capital—cereal bowl, 6¼", *TM* gold Capitol logo,
NBM, WAR 30.00
B&O—Derby—9" dinner plate, blue flower design center,
NBM, SGO 50.00
B&A—Berkshire—3½" pedestal compote, *TM* double logo,
"Boston & Albany-New York Central Lines," *NBM* 200.00
CN—Queen Elizabeth—salad plate, 5½", *TM* colorful maple
leaf emblem, *NBM, R—D* 28.50
CP—Maple Leaf Blue—9" dinner plate, *TM* blue maple leaf
border design, *NBS, MIN* 28.00
CP—Maple Leaf Brown—9¼" soup plate, *TM* brown maple
leaf border design, *NBS, LIM* 32.00
C&O—George Washington—10½" service plate, Geo.
Washington portrait, wide gold border, *BM, BUFF* 700.00
C&O—Silhouette—7 x 3¼" ashtray, Geo. Washington bust
on front, *SM, NBM, BUFF* 65.00
C&O—Chessie—9¾" dinner plate, *TM* Chessie kitten logo,
NBM, SYR 80.00
CB&Q—Violets & Daisies—5¾" plate, loose flowers,
BM, BUFF 28.00
CB&Q—Aristrocrat—7¼" plate, *TM* Burlington Route logo,
NBM, SYR 85.00
CB&Q—Chuck Wagon—Bouillon cup, *SM* "The Chuck Wagon
C-DZ," *NBM, SYR* 65.00
CMStP&P—Olympian—cup and saucer, CM&StP in cup, The
Olympian on saucer, *NBM, LEX* 125.00
CMStP&P—Peacock—double egg cup, colorful peacock motif,
MBS, SYR 18.00
CMStP&P—Traveler—demitasse cup and saucer, flying geese,
BM, SYR 38.00
C&NW—Patriot—9" dinner plate, red, blue bars, red
pinstripe border, *BM, SGO* 85.00
C&NW—400—10½" service plate, 400 diesel streamliner,
BM, SGO 550.00
CRI&P—LaSalle—5¾" x 8¼" oval dish, *RI* monogram in
green border design, *NBM, BUFF* 95.00
D&H—Adirondack—10½" plate, *TM* D&H diesel freight
and canal, *NBS, SYR* 100.00
DL&W—St. Albans—8½ " plate, floral pattern spaced
in border, *NBS, SYR* 45.00

D&RGW—Prospector—6¾" salad bowl, *TM* "Rio Grande,"
NBM, SYR 35.00
D&IR—Vermillion—9" dinner plate, Indian logo, Vermillion
Route, *NBM, SYR* 150.00
ERIE—Starucca—5¾" cereal bowl, *TM* Erie diamond logo,
blue pinstripe border, *NBM, IRO* 48.00
ERIE—Susquehana—9¾" x 5" celery, *TM* Erie diamond logo,
floral design border, *BM, BUFF* 75.00
ERIE—Gould—8¾" x 5 7/8" rectangular platter, *TM* "Erie"
in script, floral border, *NBM, SGO* 57.00
GN—Mountains & Flowers—6½" salad plate, mountains
background, flowers foreground, *BM, SYR* 30.00
GN—Glory Of The West—9" x 7" platter, mountains and
pine trees, *BM, SYR* 45.00
GN—Rocky—cereal bowl, colorful animal characters, *SM*
mountain goat logo, *NBM, SYR* .150.00
GN—Oriental—cup and saucer, flower pot design border,
BM, SYR 100.00
GM&O—Rose—8¾" soup plate, *TM* "GM&O," winged logo,
NBM, SYR 55.00
IC—French Quarter—10 5/8" service plate, "Old Grima
Home," *BM, BSH* 225.00
MEC—Kennebec—5¾" x 8¼" oval dish, *TM* "Maine Central
Railroad," *NBM, SYR* 65.00
MStP&SSM—Logan—9" dinner plate, flower design around
border, *NBM, MYR* 95.00
MStP&SSM—Banner—5½" x 7¾" oval dish, *TM* banner logo
in pinstripe border, *NBM, MDK* .85.00
MKT—Blue Bonnet—9¾" dinner plate, 2 flowers at lower
border, *BM, BUFF* 225.00
MOPAC—Eagle—5½" plate, *TM* The Eagle motif, *NBM,*
SYR 28.00
MOPAC—State Flowers—10½" service plate, *TM* steam train
center, *NBM, SYR* 195.00
MOPAC—State Capitols—10½" service plate, *TM* diesel
streamliner center, *BM, SYR* 300.00
NYC—DeWitt Clinton—9" dinner plate, *TM* DeWitt Clinton
engine 1831 in border, *BM, BUFF* 45.00
NYC—Mercury—9" dinner plate, *TM* "NYC" in 12 vertical
lines, *NBM, SYR* 27.00
NYC—Country Gardens—11" service plate, brown garden
scene center, *NBM, BUFF* 37.50
NYC—Vanderbilt—8½" x 5¾" platter, geometric border
design, *BM, BUFF* 38.00
NYC—Mohawk—10" dinner plate, *TM* "NYC" in black
stripes on pink, *NBM, SYR* 100.00

NEW HAVEN—Platinum Blue—gravy boat, nude kneeling
figure, *BM, BUFF* 55.00
NEW HAVEN—Merchants—8¾" dinner plate, *TM* steam
train, map and ship, *BM, BUFF* 75.00
N&W—Cavalier—7" salad bowl, *TM* "N&W Ry" script in
floral border, *NBM, LAMB* 45.00
NP—Monad—9" dinner plate, *TM* Monad logo, *NBM,*
SGO 48.00
NP—Yellowstone—9" dinner plate, *TM* Yellowstone Park
Line logo, *NBM, SGO* 75.00
NP—Villard—9½" plate, *TM* NP monogram in ornate
border, *NBM, SGO* 50.00

PENN—Purple Laurel—11" x 7¾" platter, pinstripe and
floral border design, *BM, STR* 32.00
PENN—Keystone—4 3/8" x 9" oval dish, *TM* Keystone logo,
brown pinstripes, *NBM, WAR* 35.00
PENN—Mountain Laurel—9¼" plate, green border, floral
spray center, *BM, SGO* 27.50
PULLMAN—Indian Tree—8¼" x 5¾" platter, *TM* "Pullman,"
Indian tree center, floral & geometric border, *NBM,*
SYR 75.00

SD&A—Carriso—9" dinner plate, *TM* logo in brown
pinstripe border, *NBM, BUFF* 200.00
SOUTHERN—Peach Blossom—7¼" plate, *TM* SR logo in
pinstripe border, *NBM, BUFF* 95.00
SP—Harriman Blue—cup, *SM* old Sunset logo, wavy blue
border, *NBM, MAD* 95.00
SP—Sunset—cup, *SM* new Sunset logo, green floral border,
NBM, SYR 85.00
SP—Sunset—10¼" dinner plate, *TM* Sunset logo, green
floral border, *BM, BUFF* 75.00
SP—Prairie Mountain Wild Flowers—9½" dinner plate,
various mountain wild flowers, *BM, SYR* 55.00

UP—Harriman Blue—5½" x 12" celery tray, wavy blue
border, *BM, SCM* 45.00
UP—Winged Streamliner—demitasse cup and saucer,
TM winged streamliner motif, *NBM, STR* 27.50
UP—Overland—7¼" x 3½" pickle tray, *TM* UP shield logo,
miniature western scenes in border, *BM, SGO* 85.00
UP—Challenger—6½" plate, *TM* "The Challenger,"
NBM, SYR 20.00

WABASH—Banner—5½" plate, *TM* flag logo, *NBM,*
SYR 65.00
WP—Feather Fiver—5½" plate, *TM* "Feather River Route,"
red feather design, *NBM, SGO* 30.00

Flatware

SILVER FLATWARE

Flatware pieces are listed by Railroad, then by Pattern Name. More extensive pattern information can be found in Dominy & Morganfruh's *A Collector's Guide To Railroad Flatware.*

Key to abbreviations:
TM—Top marked
SM—Side marked
BM—Bottom marked
HH—Hollow handle

Silver manufacturers
GOR—Gorham
INT'L —International
MER.BR.—Meridian Britannia
R&B—Reed & Barton

AT&SF RY—Cromwell, demitasse spoon, *TM* "AT&SF RY," *INT'L* 22.00
SANTA FE—Albany, teaspoon, *BM* "Santa Fe," *GOR* 10.00
ACL—Zephry, bouillon spoon, *TM* "ACL," *INT'L* 12.00
B&O—Cromwell, teaspoon, *TM* "B&O" script, *R&B* 15.00
CCC&StL RY—Alden,teaspoon,*TM* "CCC&StL RY," *R&B* .30.00
CGW RY—Clarendon, teaspoon, *TM* "CGW RY" script, *R&B* 35.00
CMStP&P RR—Broadway, soup spoon, *BM* "CMStP&P RR," *INT'L* 15.00
C&NW RY—Modern Art, dinner knife, *HH, BM* "C&NW RY" script, *R&B* 20.00
CStPM&O RY—Modern Art, dinner knife, *HH, BM* "CStPM&O Ry" script, *R&B* 25.00
D&H.Royal, dinner knife, *TM* "The D&H," *R&B* 20.00
D&RGW RR—Belmont, teaspoon, *TM* "D&RGW RR," *R&B* 25.00
ERIE—Elmwood, soup spoon, *TM* logo, *GOR* 20.00
FEC RY—Cromwell, oyster fork, *TM* "FEC RY," *INT'L* 18.00
GM&O—Broadway, dinner fork, *TM*, "GM&O," *INT'L* . . .*14.00*

GN—Hutton, demitasse spoon, *TM* "GN," *INT'L* 16.00
GN—Hutton, dinner fork, *TM* "GN," *INT'L* 12.00
GN—Hutton, dinner knife, *TM* "GN," *INT'L* 12.00
GN—Hutton, tablespoon, *TM* "GN," *INT'L* 12.00
GN—Hutton, teaspoon, *TM* "GN," *INT'L* 10.00
ICRR—Alden, teaspoon, *TM* ornate monogram, *R&B* 18.00
LACKAWANNA—Cromwell, iced teaspoon, *TM*
  "Lackawanna," *INT'L* 22.00
NC&StL—Sierra, dinner fork, *BM* "NC&StL," *R&B* 16.00
NYC—Century, dessert fork, *BM* "NYC," *INT'L* 12.00
NYC—Century, grapefruit spoon, *BM* "NYC," *INT'L* 12.00
NYC—Century, iced teaspoon, *BM* "NYC," *INT'L* 16.00
NPR—Alden, dinner fork, *TM* logo, *R&B* 22.00
NPR—Alden, soup spoon, *TM* logo, *R&B* 20.00
NPR—Winthrop, dinner knife, ornate *HH, TM* "NPR" script,
  GOR 26.00
NPR—Winthrop, iced teaspoon, *TM* "NPR" script,
  GOR 22.00
NORTHERN PACIFIC RAILWAY COMPANY—Silhouette,
  butter knife, *BM* full name, *INT'L* 15.00
PRR—Kings Alternate, dessert fork, *TM* Keystone logo,
  INT'L 28.00
PULLMAN—Roosevelt, tablespoon, *BM* "Pullman,"
  INT'L 15.00
ROCK ISLAND LINES—Albany, dinner fork, *HH, TM* RI
  monogram, *INT'L* 15.00
SEABOARD—Albany, butter knife, *HH, TM* "Seaboard,"
  INT'L 15.00
SEABOARD—Albany, grapefruit spoon, *TM* "Seaboard,"
  INT'L 10.00
SEABOARD—Albany, pickle fork, *TM* "Seaboard,"
  INT'L 12.00
SOO LINE—Sussex, iced teaspoon, *TM* logo, *INT'L* 35.00
SOO LINE—Sussex, tablespoon, *TM* logo, *INT'L* 30.00
SOUTHERN—Sierra, sugar tongs, *SM* "Southern,"
  R&B 15.00
SOUTHERN PACIFIC—Broadway, dinner fork, *BM* "Southern
  Pacific," script, *INT'L* 12.00
SOUTHERN PACIFIC—Broadway, teaspoon, *BM* Southern
  Pacific," script, *INT'L* 12.00
S.P.CO.—Westfield, teaspoon, *TM* "S.P.CO." script,
  MER.BR. 15.00
SP&S RY—Embassy, dinner knife, *BM* "SP&S RY,"
  R&B 16.00
SP&S RY—Embassy, soup spoon, *BM* "SP&S RY,"
  R&B 16.00

UPRR—Zephyr, oyster fork, *BM* "UPRR" script, *INT'L* 12.00
UPRR—Zephyr, teaspoon, *BM* "UPRR" script, *INT'L* 10.00
WESTERN PACIFIC—Hutton, tablespoon, *BM* logo,
INT'L 14.00

SILVER HOLLOWARE

ACL—covered sugar, 8 oz., *BM* "ACL," *MER.BR.* 75.00
B & M RR—covered sugar, 6 oz., *BM* "B&M RR,"
MER. BR. 65.00
CM&StP—bowl 5" diameter ornate border design, *BM*
"CM&StP" script, *R&B* 65.00
CStPM&O RY—footed toothpick holder 3¼" high, *BM*
"CStPM&O RY" script, *R&B* 75.00
C&NW RY—coffee pot, 14 oz. winged finial, *BM* "C&NW RY"
script, *INT'L* 85.00
GN—coffee pot, 14 oz., *BM* "Great Northern Ry,"
INT'L 55.00
GN—syrup w/attached drip tray, *BM* "Great Northern Ry,"
INT'L 65.00
GN—footed cakestand, beaded lattice edging, *BM* "Great
Northern Ry," *MER. BR.* 165.00

Holloware

GN—coffee pot, 8 oz. beaded edging, *SM* GNR fancy
monogram, *BM* "Great Northern Ry.," *MER.BR* 85.00
GN—caster stand w/2 cruets, *SM* "GN," *BM* "Great
Northern Ry.," *INT'L* 125.00
GN—butter chip, 3½" diameter, *TM* "GN," *BM* "Great
Northern Ry.," *INT'L* 28.00
GM&O—water pitcher, 4 pt., hinged cover, *BM* "GM&O,"
INT'L 120.00

ICRR—covered sugar, 6 oz., *SM* ICRR fancy monogram,
INT'L 85.00
LACKAWANNA—covered sugar, 8 oz., *BM* "Lackawanna,"
INT'L 75.00
L&N—sauce boat, *BM* "L&N," *INT'L* 45.00
M&StLRR—water bottle in silver frame, *BM* lid-"M&StLRR,"
R&B 275.00
NYC LINES—covered sugar, 8 oz., *BM* "NYC LINES,"
R&B 55.00
NP RY—crumb scraper 12¼" long, *BM* "NP RY" script,
1847 Rogers Bros 40.00
NPR—coffee pot, 1 pt. ornate gooseneck, *SM* Logo, *BM*
"NPR," *R&B* 110.00
NPR—sugar & creamer, pair, Pagoda style, *SM* Logo,
BM "NPR," *R&B* 150.00

Glassware

NPR—bouillion cup holder, *BM* "Northern Pacific Railway
Co.," *INT'L* 40.00
PRR—ice bowl, *SM* Keystone logo, *INT'L* 65.00
ROCK ISLAND LINES—caster stand, 3 glass shakers, *BM*
"Rock Island Lines," *INT'L* 47.50
SOO LINE—soda bottle holder, *TM* banner logo, *GOR* . . .55.00
SOO LINE—bread tray, 13¼" x 6", *TM* banner logo,
GOR 125.00
SOO LINE—coffee pot, 7/8 Pt. goose neck, *SM* banner
logo, *GOR* 125.00
SOO LINE—coffee pot, 8 oz., *BM* "Soo Line," *R&B* 68.00
SOUTHERN PACIFIC—change tray, passenger train across
center, *BM* "Southern Pacific," script, *R&B* 150.00
SOUTHERN PACIFIC—pair salt & peppers, *SM* winged logo,
BM "Southern Pacific," script, *INT'L* 75.00

UPRR—menu stand w/2 pencil holders, *BM* "UPRR," script,
INT'L 37.50
UPRR—butter pat, *BM* "UPRR," *INT'L* 25.00
WABASH—covered sugar, 14 oz., *SM* ornate "W,"
BM "Wabash," *R&B* 85.00

GLASSWARE

BN—mug, clear, "BN Burlington Northern" green,
"Transportation Needs You" 1972, black 9.50
C&O—tumbler, "C&O For Progress," in blue 8.00
CN—sherbert, cut glass stem, pinched sides, "Canadian
National Railways" frosted logo on side 35.00
D&H—water glass, thick bottom, "The D&H" etched old style
logo 25.00
FRISCO—tumbler, Frisco logo in blue 6.00
GN—cruet, clear glass, etched Great Northern Railway
goat logo 95.00
GN—cruet, clear glass, frosted older goat logo 135.00
IC—wine glass, stemmed, clear, frosted IC diamond
logo 15.00
IC—old fashion glass, large w/train 6.00
MOPAC—milk bottle, ½ pint, Missouri Pacific buzz-saw logo
one side, "Sunnymeade Farm, Bismarck, Mo." other
side 7.50
MOPAC—milk bottle, quart, buzz-saw logo, clear 12.50
NYC SYSTEM—stemmed cordial, 4¼", gold New York
Central System logo 10.00
NP—cordial, 3¾", etched Yellowstone Park logo 25.00
NP—water glass, black and red monad logo 8.00
NP—pair salt & peppers, clear glass, ornate silver tops
marked "No. Pac. Ry." 30.00
NP—milk bottle, ½ pint, embossed "Northern Pacific Railway,
Dairy and Poultry Farm, Kent. Wn." 25.00
PRR—high ball glass, large, w/red Keystone and diesel
locomotive 6.00
SANTA FE—tumbler, clear, etched "Santa Fe" in
script 5.00
SOO LINE—syrup, cut glass, silver handle and lid marked
"Soo Line" 150.00
UP—shot glass, clear, etched Union Pacific shield
logo 5.50
UP—tumbler, clear, frosted Union Pacific shield logo 6.50
UP—cocktail set, mixer, 4 glass, clear, frosted Union
Pacific shield logo on each 26.00

MENUS

AMTRAK—"Good Morning" club breakfast, single card
7" x 11", recent 1.00
AT&SF—"The Chief" dinner, 1939, red monogram on
cover 5.50
AT&SF—"The Grand Canyon Ltd." luncheon, 1940, gold
monogram on cover 6.00
BURLINGTON ROUTE—"Zephyr" luncheon, 1943, Zephyr
streamliner cover 5.50
CANADIAN PACIFIC—"The Dominion" dinner, 1952, Peggy
Cove scene cover 5.00
C&NW—"400" dinner, Dec. 1954, "Season's Greetings,"
pioneer locomotive scene on cover 6.50
C&NW—"Northwestern Limited" supper and wine list, Sept.
'05, football player on cover 18.00
C&NW—"Famous Trains," supper, with today's special insert
page, 12-1-09, couple seated at table on cover 20.00
GREAT NORTHERN—"Empire Builder," breakfast, 1936,
"Riding Black Horse," Indian chief, on cover,
colorful 22.50
FRED HARVEY—Union Terminal, Cleveland, dinner,
June 20, 1939, 1876 dining table scene on cover 4.50
ILLINOIS CENTRAL—"Centennial" luncheon, single card
8" x 11", Centennial medallion 1851-1951 depicted
upper right 2.50
ILLINOIS CENTRAL—"Panama Limited" breakfast, 1963,
transition of locomotives, Iron Horse to modern
diesel 2.00

Uncommon menus

LEHIGH VALLEY—"Black Diamond Express" dinner, 1927, chef and Black Diamond Express on cover 25.00

MILWAUKEE ROAD—"The Hiawatha" luncheon, 1962, Thunderbird design on cover 5.00

NEW YORK CENTRAL—"Empire State Express," luncheon, 1939, new streamlined 20th Century Ltd. on cover 7.50

NP—Special excursion, St. Paul Jobber's Union, dinner and wine list, 1885, litho. of Indian maiden front cover, dining car back cover, (rare) 45.00

NP—Casserole shape, 4 pages, luncheon, 1911, dining car table setting on back cover 15.00

NP—Apple shape, 4 pages, breakfast, 1914, dining car table setting on back cover 15.00

NP—Baked potato shape, 4 pages, dinner, 1914, dining car kitchen scene on back cover .20.00

ROCK ISLAND—"Route Of The Rockets" luncheon, Dec. 1945, red Rocket and steam locomotive on cover, holly sprig 7.50

SEABOARD—breakfast, 1943, WWII, flag and soldier blowing bugle on cover 4.50

SOUTHERN PACIFIC—special "Anzar Temple Pilgrimage" luncheon, June 1925, couple seated at dining car table 25.00

UNION PACIFIC—"Domeliner" City Of Los Angeles, breakfast, 1971, Fremont St., Las Vegas on cover 1.50

WESTERN PACIFIC-RIO GRANDE-BURLINGTON— Chicago Democratic Convention 2 pages, July 10, 1940, cartoon characters of donkey & bear on cover. Tied with red, white, blue ribbon 22.50

TABLECLOTHS

BALTIMORE & OHIO—Capitol logo center, floral design border woven in, white on white, 34" x 34" 15.00

BURLINGTON ROUTE—logo stamped in black near edge, white, 35" x 35" 10.00

C&NW—Chicago Northwestern Line logo and "CStPM&O RY" below, overall fleur-de-lis design woven in, white on white, 54" x 68" 22.50

ROCK ISLAND—large logo at center, floral design around, woven in, white on white, 34" x 33" 12.00

SOO LINE—logo at center, woven in, white on white, 34" x 34" 18.00

UNION PACIFIC—"UP RR" woven small near edge, roses woven in, rose pink, 50" x 42" 10.00

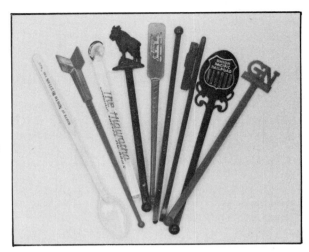

Stir sticks

NAPKINS

BURLINGTON ROUTE—logo at center woven in, white
on white, 18½" x 21" 8.00
C&NW—Chicago & Northwestern Line logo at center, floral
border design woven in, white on white, 22" x 22" 12.00
FRISCO LINES—name woven into fancy floral design each
corner, white on white, 22" x 20½" 8.00
GREAT NORTHERN RY—logo at center, woven in, white
on white, 22" x 21" 9.50
MILWAUKEE ROAD—Hiawatha emblem printed in corner,
plain border, magenta on tan, 10¾" x 16½" 8.00
NORTHERN PACIFIC RY—Monad logo at center, plain
border, woven in, white on tan, 20" x 21" 7.50
NORTHERN PACIFIC RY—Yellowstone Park Line logo at
center, woven in, red-brown on tan, 13" x 18" 10.00
SOUTHERN PACIFIC LINES—Sunset logo at center, fancy
border with poppies woven in, white on white,
21" x 21" 15.00
UNION PACIFIC—"UP RR" woven small near edge, rose
pink, 19½" x 20½" 6.00

STIR STICKS

AMTRAK—plastic, blue, arrow top 1.00
B&O—iron, in form of golf club 7.50
BURLINGTON ROUTE—plastic, white, dome car
cut-out 7.00

C&NW—plastic, white, "Route of the 400," spoon
tip 5.00
GN—plastic, "Empire Builder," goat at top 3.00
GN—plastic, red, "Western Star," goat at top 5.00
GN—plastic, "The Growing Great Northern," modern
goat 2.00
GN—plastic, "From Ranch of Empire Builder" on
rod 5.00
GN—plastic, ball top, "Great Northern Railway" on
rod 1.50
HIAWATHA—"Nothing finer on rails," clear glass,
spoon tip 15.00
SP—plastic, green, "Your Friendly Railroad,"
paddle 4.50
SP—plastic, red, ball top 4.00
UP—plastic, red, "Golden Spike Centennial,"
1869-1969 . . . . 1.50
UP—plastic, red, gold shield log top 1.50

MISCELLANEOUS

AMTRAK—Coaster, plastic backed paper, round with
scalloped edges, Amtrak logo at center, blue, red
and white 0.25
AMTRAK—Napkin, paper, logo and slogan "We've Been
Working On The RAILROAD!" blue, red and
white 0.25
BN—Napkin, paper, BN logo, green and white 0.50
SOO LINE—Napkin, paper, white, red logo with red
wavy border 1.00
UP—Coaster, cardboard, round with scalloped edges,
cocktail glass depicted in center, yellow and
red 0.75
UP—Coaster, cardboard, round with scalloped edges,
winged streamliner motif in center, surrounded by
slogan "Route Of The Daily Domeliners" blue and
white 0.50
UP—Toothpick—two sealed in paper wrapper marked with
blue Union Pacific shield logo 0.25

KEYS

Switch keys have always been popular with the railroadiana collector. Thousands of them were made down through the years of

bronze or brass, some of steel or iron. The railroad's name or initials were stamped on the front side of the bow. The letter S (Switch) or other Department letters and a serial number, along with the maker's mark, were stamped on the back side. Many collectors suspect that switch keys found without a serial number and maker's hallmark, having only railroad initials stamped on them, are possible fakes. Fully marked switch keys, especially from early defunct railroads, bring the highest prices.

There were many other railroad marked keys in use for locks on shanties, coal sheds, signal boxes, cabooses, coaches and so on. These various keys are different in size and shape from the regular switch key and are also being collected. Many recent caboose or coach keys are marked "Adlake" only, and these do not bring the price of those that are railroad marked.

SWITCH (Brass unless otherwise noted)

A C L RR.—"#19127, Fraim" in banner 18.00
A T & S F RY.—"S, 13679, Adlake" 16.00
B & O—"C. 33498, Fraim" in banner, long barrel 13.00
B & O RR—"S. 148314" 15.00
B & M RR—"Bohannan" 16.00
B N INC.—"Adlake," unused 8.50
B R & P R.R.—"S, A & W Co." 25.00
BURLINGTON ROUTE—"S, 8753, A & W Co.," steel
    key 18.50

Switch keys

BURLINGTON ROUTE—"S, 228243, A & W CO." 16.50
C C C & St.L.R.R.—"S, X-8782-B, A & W Co." 18.50
C G W—"Adlake," unused 16.00
C M & P S R.R.—"Loeffelholtz" 35.00
C M & St.P. RY.—"Loeffelholtz" 18.00
C M & St.P. RY .—"B," steel key 20.00
C M & St.P. & P.—"F-S Hdwe." 12.50
C N RR—"S, Adlake" 15.00
C N R—"Adlake," unused 13.00
C & NW R.R.—"Bohannan" 20.00
C & NW RY.—"S, A & W Co." 18.00
C & O—"18211, Adlake," unused 14.00
C R I & P RR.—"S, 37860, A & W Co." 12.50
C.St.P. M & O RY.—"S. Slaymaker" 22.50
C. St.P. M & O RY.—"S, A & W Co." 25.00
C & S—"4821, Adlake" 35.00
C & W I RR—"S, A & W Co." 25.00
C & W M RR.—"S, A & W Co." 60.00
D & H Co.—"S, 1533," huge letters 16.00
D L & W—"Fraim" in Keystone 16.50
D & I R RR.—"S, 356," steel, "oiler" key 35.00
D & R G—"S, 475," unused, huge letters 18.00
D M & I R—"4674, Adlake" 25.00
D M & N R—"S, 082, A & W" 45.00
E J & E RY.—"S, 8979, Adlake" 17.00
E R R—"Slaight," small key 25.00
ERIE RR—"F-S Hdwe." 12.50
E L RR—"Adlake," fairly recent 12.50
F & P M RR.—"J.L. Howard," small key 45.00
F D D M & S—"Fraim" in Keystone 38.50
F W & D C—"Adlake" 27.50
FRISCO—"Adlake" 15.00
G T W—"Adlake," unused 16.00
G N RY.—"Fraim" in Keystone 16.50
G B & W RR—"W 110" 40.00
H B L RR—"968, Slaymaker" 14.00
I C RR—"S, 75793, Adlake" 12.50
I H B—"Adlake" 16.00
I H B RR—"Adlake" 18.00
K C P & G—"Bohannan" 30.00
K C S RY—"10284," huge fancy marking 17.50
K & I T—"1634, Adlake" 22.50
L V R.R.—"S, A & W" 18.00
L & N E—"Adlake" 40.00
L & N RR.—"D, 39976, Dayton," fat short barrel 16.00

M & I—N P R—"Fraim" in Keystone, double marked 45.00
M & O RR—"Bohannan" 33.00
M & St.L. RR.—"S, 0152, Bohannan" 28.50
MOPAC RR.—"37325, F-S Hdwe." .12.50
M H C & W RR.—"Bohannan" 38.00
M K & T RY.—"Fraim" in banner, fat short barrel 20.00
N Y C S—"Adlake" 13.00
N Y O & W RR—"13760, Adlake" 35.00
N P RR.—"S, Slaymaker" 18.00
N P RY.—"Adlake" 16.50
OMAHA—"Adlake" 22.50

Miscellaneous coach, signal, and general use keys

O R & N CO—"A & W Co., R & B 586" 46.00
P R R—"F-S Hdwe.," knobs around hilt 22.00
P & P U RY.—"466, Adlake" 36.00
P & L E—"862-B, F.S. Hdwe." 18.00
P T R A—"Adlake" 17.00
R F & P—"Climax" 22.50
RUTLAND—"Adlake" 25.00
RDG CO.—"Adlake" 15.00
St.L & S.F. RR.—"S, A & W Co." 25.00
St.L & S W RR.—"Slaymaker" 31.00
St.P M & M RR.—"S" 50.00
SANTA FE—"S, 29636, A & W Co." 14.50
SOO LINE—"S, A & W Co." 22.00
S P CO.—"CS-4-S, Adlake" 11.50

S P CO.—"CS-44, Special 5693" 15.00
S P CO.—"Freight, A & W Co." 15.00
S P RY.—Huge letters, long barrel 16.00
T & P RY.—"10414, Adlake" 22.75
T P & W—"922, Adlake" 22.50
T R R A—"9918, Adlake" 28.50
U P—"28840, Adlake," unused, crude, recent 10.00
U P RR.—"F.S. Hdwe Co." 15.00
U S T V A—"814, Fraim" in banner 14.00
V RR.—"S, 5884," ornate, big letters 35.00
VGN RR.—"Adlake" 30.00
W C RY.—"Loeffelholtz" 28.00
W M RY.—"11165, Adlake" 15.00
W P RR.—"Adlake," unused 15.00
W & St.P. R.R.—"S. Wilson, Bohannan" 65.00

Caboose, Coach & Miscellaneous (Brass unless otherwise noted)

ACL—"Adlake," long solid barrel, caboose 10.00
B & O RR—"B, No. 107," long hollow barrel, coach 18.00
C N R—"Mitchell," long hollow barrel, coach 15.00
C N R—"Mitchell," long solid barrel, caboose 12.00
C M & St. P RR—"STORE DEPT.," short hollow barrel,
  switch key type 24.00
C M & St.P RR—"BCC" (baggage car cellar), short
  hollow barrel switch key type 28.00
GN—Short solid barrel, shanty 9.50
NP—"Adlake," long solid barrel, iron key, coach 10.00
NP RY.—"Loeffelholz, U.S. MAIL CAR," small key,
  double bit, hollow barrel 30.00
M & St.L RR—"ROAD DEPT.," small switch key type,
  hollow barrel 35.00
P R R—"Y65," short hollow barrel, iron key, general
  use 6.00
P RR—"Yale," flat key, signal use 7.50
UP—"Adlake," long solid barrel, caboose 10.00
W RY—"Adlake," long solid barrel, caboose 12.00
Unmarked—"Adlake," long solid barrel, caboose 5.00

LAMPS

The classification lamps displayed at the front of the steam
locomotives, the marker lamps that hung on the rear of the

caboose or tail end of the Express trains, the signal lamps used on switch-stands, the interior lamps used in the caboose and coaches, and the track-walker's and inspector's lamps, all are being collected today. These bring top prices when found in their all-original condition, bearing a railroad marking. The oil-burning switch-stand lamp appears to be the most popular with the collector.

CLASSIFICATION LAMPS, STEAM LOCOMOTIVE ERA

A pair of these lamps was displayed on the front of the locomotive to indicate its running classification. Each lamp is equipped with a cast iron arm for mounting in the bracket.

"CM&StP RY"—no maker's mark, flat top, electric, two
   clear lens, inside hand changeable colored glass
   panes 100.00
"EJ&E RY—Dressel," dome top, oil, two clear lens, inside
   hand changeable colored glass panes 150.00
"GN RY—Pyle National, 1924," diver's helmet type, electric,
   two clear lens, flip levers to change inner color green
   lens 125.00
M SO RR—Adlake," dome top, oil, three clear lens,
   inside hand changeable colored glass panes 175.00

Engine classification lamps—oil and electric

Tail end marker lamps—oil burning

MARKER LAMPS, STEAM ERA

A pair of these was displayed at the tail end of passenger or freight trains to indicate their classification. A cast iron mounting arm is attached at bottom.

"CPR—H.L. Piper," dome top, oil, two red, two green
 bulls-eye lens, passenger car 115.00
"C&NW RY—Adlake," square top, oil, two red, two green
 bulls-eye lens, caboose 100.00
CRI&P RR—Handlan," dome top, oil, one red, two green
 bulls-eye lens, passenger car 115.00
GN RY—Dressel," dome top, oil, two red, two green
 bulls-eye lens, passenger car 125.00
"NP—Adlake," square top, oil, one red, three amber
 bulls-eye lens, caboose 100.00

SWITCH—STAND LAMPS, STEAM ERA

These were mounted on the iron switch-stand post. Each lamp has four lenses, a combination of two red, two green or two amber. Metal discs or targets of matching colors are sometimes displayed around the lense. The inside oil burning pot is usually missing when found.

"C&NW—Dressel," dome top, oil, square post style mount base, four prongs 95.00

"CM&StP RY—Star Lantern Co., 1906," fluted top, oil, rectangular post mount base 110.00

"DM&I R—"Adlake," square top, oil, bell bottom, fork style mount base with four colored metal targets 125.00

"GN RY—Adlake," square top, oil, fork style mount base, two holes 115.00

"SOO LINE—Armspear," dome top, brass, square post style mount based, four prongs 135.00

Switch stand lamps

SEMAPHORE LAMPS, STEAM ERA

These were located behind the metal or wood signal blades at top of the semaphore poles to illuminate the colored lenses.

"GN RR—Adlake," oil, fuel pot intact, single clear bulls-eye lens 95.00

"NP—Adlake," electric, single clear bulls-eye lens 65.00

"UP—Adlake," electric, double clear bulls-eye lens 75.00

INSPECTOR'S AND TRACK-WALKER'S LAMPS

Inspector's lamps were used by railroad workers to check the journal boxes on rolling stock. The track-walker's lamp is much the same except it has a red lens at the rear.

"CM&StP RY—Star Lantern Co., Pat. 1910," car inspector,
kerosene 100.00
"UP RR—C.T.Ham, Pat.1909," track-walker, kerosene, red
lens at rear 115.00
"UNMARKED—Dietz," no patent date, car inspector,
kerosene 45.00
"UNMARKED—Oxweld, 1926," car inspector, carbide
lamp 75.00
"UNMARKED—Dietz, pat. 1909," track-walker, kerosene,
red lens at rear 85.00

**Caboose
wall lamp**

WALL LAMPS

There were many special design wall lamps for the caboose and
passenger cars. Examples are listed here alphabetically by
manufacturer.

ADAMS& WESTLAKE—coach, side wall lamp, round
kerosene fount, tall glass chimney, orante brass bracket
arm, 20" tall. Early 150.00
ALADDIN—caboose, brass fuel pot, wall mount arm, glass
chimney, mantle and parchment shade. Complete 50.00
HANDLAN—caboose, model 50, ball type fuel pot, glass
chimney, metal shade, mounting back plate with
chimney holder, 18" tall 95.00
JOHNSON, URBANA—caboose, tinware fuel pot, glass
chimney, metal backplate for wall mounting, metal smoke
deflector, 21" tall 65.00

SAFETY CO. N.Y.—caboose, brass candle lamp, complete
with 5½" tall glass chimney and wall mount
bracket 45.00
UNMARKED—coach, Pullman berth lamp, wall, electric,
9" tall, metal, half-round milk white globe with clear
opening at side 35.00
UNMARKED—coach, Pullman, berth lamp, wall, electric,
9" tall, brass, white plastic shade 55.00

Inspector's
lamp

LANTERNS

The earliest lanterns used were the whale-oil type, with no
special features. Gradually they were modified to railroad
specifications. The railroads identified their lanterns by having
their names stamped or embossed somewhere on the frame and
also etched or embossed on the globe. The manufacturer's name
and patent dates are also found on most lanterns. The earlier
lanterns came with tall globes; later ones had short globes. An all
original lantern with the railroad's name on both frame and
globe brings the higher price. A restored lantern with an unmat-
ched or unmarked globe is priced lower. Battery-powered

lanterns today have replaced these oil-burning lanterns of yesteryear.

Conductor's lanterns are high on the collector's list and usually are sold at auction. They are all brass or nickel plated and generally smaller in size than the switchman's lantern. The globe is clear or sometimes two color, such as half green and half clear. They are not railroad marked unless they were presentation pieces, with the name of the railroad and conductor on the globe or frame. Conductor's lanterns are rare.

Key to abbreviations:
P—P after year is the last patent date shown on frame
NPD—No patent dates on frame
BB—Bell bottom
EMB—Embossed letters
TOB—Twist off bottom

SWITCHMEN'S HAND LANTERNS

"A&StL RR"—embossed on globe, whale oil type, ca. 1850 ....500.00
"AT&SF RY"—(lid) "Handlan, 1928" *P*, red 3¼" globe, etched "AT&SF RY" 48.00
"AT&SF RY"—(lid) "Adams & Westlake Co. 1933" *P*, clear 3¼" globe, *EMB* "AT&SF RY" 95.00
"B&O RR LOCO"—(lid) "Adams & Westlake Co., Adlake Reliable, 1913" *P*, clear 5 3/8" globe *EMB* with capitol dome logo and "LOCO" at rear 185.00
"B&O RR"—(lid) Keystone, the "Casey," "1903" *P*, clear 5 3/8" globe *EMB* with capitol dome logo 125.00
"B&A RR"—(lid) "Dietz No. 6," *BB*, *NPD*, clear 5 7/8" globe *EMB* "B&A RR." Pot slips out from bottom 150.00
"B&M RR"—(lid) "Adams & Westlake Co., Adlake Reliable, 1913" *P*, clear 5 3/8" globe, *EMB* "B&M RR" 75.00
"BR&P RY"—(lid) "C.T. Ham," *BB*, "1889" *P*, clear 5 3/8" globe *EMB* "BR&P RY." Pot slips out from bottom 145.00
"BURLINGTON ROUTE"—(lid) "A & W Adlake Reliable, 1913" *P*, clear 5 3/8" globe, *EMB* BURLINGTON ROUTE logo 85.00
"BR"—(lid) "Adlake Kero, 1959" *P*, clear 3¼" globe, unmarked 40.00
"CNR—(lid) "Hiram L. Piper, 1955" *P*, clear 3¼" globe, etched "C.N.R." 36.00

"C&O"—(dome) "Adams & Westlake Co., 1945" *P,* clear 3¼"
globe, etched "C&O" 30.00
"CGW RR"—(lid) "Adams & Westlake Co., Adlake Reliable,
1913" *P,* red 5 3/8" globe, *EMB* "CGW RR" 100.00
"C&NW RY"—(dome) "Adams & Westlake Co., Adlake 250
Kero, 1923" *P,* clear 3¼" globe, etched "C&NW" 38.00
"C&NW RY"—(lid) "Adams & Westlake Co., Adlake Reliable,
1913" *P,* clear 5 3/8" globe, *EMB* "C&NW RY" in
rectangle 62.00
"C&NW RY"—(lid) "Adlake Reliable, 1923" *P,* clear 5 3/8"
globe *EMB* THE NORTHWESTERN LINE logo and
"CStPM&O RY" below "SAFETY FIRST" at rear 150.00
"CM&StP RY"—(lid) brass top, *BB,* "Adams & Westlake
Co., clear 5 3/8" globe *EMB* "CM&StP RY" 135.00
"CM&StP RY"—(lid) "Armspear, 1913" *P,* clear 5 3/8" globe
EMB "CM&StP RY" 60.00
"CM&StP RY"—(dome) "Adlake 250 Kero, 1923" *P,* red
3¼" globe etched "CM&StP" 38.00
"CMStP&P RR"—(lid) "Adams & Westlake Co. 1934", *P,* green
3¼" globe etched "CMStP&P RR" 40.00
"CStPM&O RY"—(lid) "Adams & Westlake Co., Adlake
Reliable, 1913" *P,* clear 5 3/8" globe *EMB* "CStPM&O"
in rectangle 125.00
CStPM&O RY"—(dome) "Adams & Westlake Co., Adlake 250
Kero, 1923" *P,* clear 3¼" globe, unmarked 45.00
"CCC&StL RY"—(lid) "Dietz Vesta, 1929" *P,* clear 4¼" globe
EMB "CCC&StL RY" 45.00
"D&H CO"—(lid) "Adams & Westlake Co., Adlake Reliable,
1913" *P,* clear 5 3/8" globe *EMB* THE D & H logo 150.00
"DL&W RR"—(lid) "Dressel, 1913" *P,* clear 5 3/8" globe
EMB "DL&W RR" 135.00
"D&RG RR"—(lid) "Adams & Westlake Co., The Adams,
1909" *P,* clear 5 3/8" globe *EMB* "D&RG RR" large
in rectangle 125.00
"D&IR RR"—(lid) "Adams & Westlake Co., Adlake 250
Kero, 1923" *P,* amber 3¼" globe unmarked 55.00
"D&IR RR"—(lid) "Adams & Westlake Co., Adlake
Reliable, 1913" *P,* clear, 5 3/8" globe etched
"D&I RR" 145.00
"DM&N RY"—(lid) "Adams & Westlake Co., 1895" *P,* clear
5 3/8" globe *EMB* "DM&N RY" 175.00
"DM&N RY"—(lid) "Adams & Westlake Co., Adlake
Reliable," *BB,* 1912" *P,* red 5 3/8" globe *EMB*
"DM&N RY" 185.00
"ERIE RR"—(lid) "C.T. Ham, 39 Railroad, 1893" *P,* clear
5¾" globe *EMB* "E RR Co," *TOB* 75.00

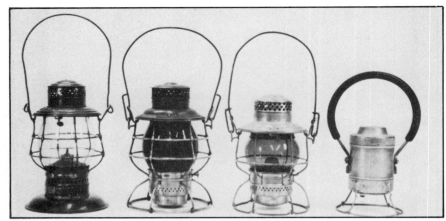

Switchmen's hand lanterns

"GN RY"—(lid) "Armspear, 1925" *P,* clear 3¼" globe *EMB*
"G N RY" 50.00
"GN RY"—(lid) "Adams & Westlake Co., Adlake 250
Kero, 1923" *P,* clear 3¼" globe unmarked. 35.00
"GN RY"—(lid) Adams & Westlake, The Adams, 1909" *P,*
clear 5 3/8" globe *EMB* "GN RY, SAFETY ALWAYS"
at rear, *TOB* 75.00
"GN RY"—(lid) "Adams & Westlake Co., Adlake Reliable,
1913" *P,* amber 5 3/8" globe etched "GN RY, SAFETY
ALWAYS" at rear 75.00
"IC RR"—(lid) "Adams & Westlake Co., The Adams,
1889" *P,* clear 5 3/8" globe *EMB* "IC RR" in rectangle,
TOB 75.00
"IC RR"—(dome) "Adams & Westlake Co., Adlake 250
Kero, 1923" *P,* red 3¼" globe etched "IC RR" 45.00
"K&IT RR"—(lid) "Dressel," *NPD,* red 3¼" globe
unmarked 45.00
"LS&MS RY"—(lid) "Adams & Westlake Co., Adlake
Reliable, 1913" *P,* clear 5 3/8" globe *EMB* "LS & MS RY,"
TOB 95.00
"LV RR"—(lid) "RR signal L&L Co., 1889" *P,* clear
5 3/8" globe *EMB* "LV RR" *TOB* 125.00
"MC RR"—(lid) "Armspear, 1889" *P,* clear 5 3/8" globe
EMB "MC RR," *TOB* 100.00
"M&StL RR"—(dome) "Adams & Westlake Co., Adlake 250
Kero, 1923" *P,* red 3¼" globe etched "M&StL RR" 65.00
"M&StL RR"—(lid) "Armspear, 1913" *P,* clear 5 3/8" globe
EMB "M&StL RR" 125.00

94

"M&StL RR"—(lid) Keystone, "Casey, 1903" *P,* clear 5 3/8"
globe *EMB* "M&StL RR" 145.00
"MOPAC"—(lid) 'Handlan," *NPD,* clear 5 3/8" globe *EMB*
"M.P." *TOB* 65.00
"MOPAC"—(on BB) brass top, "Handlan Buck," *NPD,*
clear 5 3/8" globe *EMB* "M.P., SAFETY FIRST" at
rear 125.00
"NEW YORK CENTRAL"—(lid) "Dietz No. 6," *BB, NPD,* red
5 7/8" globe *EMB* "NEW YORK CENTRAL 95.00
"NYC RR"—(lid) "Adams & Westlake Co., Adlake
Reliable, 1913" *P,* clear 5 3/8" globe *EMB*
"NYC RR" 55.00
"NYLE&W RR"—(lid) "Adams & Westlake Co., The Adams,
1889" *P,* clear 5½" globe *EMB* "NYLE&W RR,"
TOB 135.00
"NYNH&H RR"—(lid) Dietz Vesta, 1944" *P,* clear 4¼"
globe *EMB* "NYNH&H RR" 36.00
"NYNH&H RR"—(lid) "Adams & Westlake Co., Adlake
Reliable, 1913" *P,* clear 5 3/8" globe *EMB*
"NYNH&H RR" 95.00
"NC RY"—(lid) "R.R. Signal L&L Co., 1897" *P,* clear 5½"
globe *EMB* "NCR," *TOB* 150.00
"NP RY"—(lid) "Adams & Westlake Co., 1938" *P,* green
3¼" globe etched "NP RY" 45.00
"NP RR"—(lid) "Adams & Westlake Co., The Adams,
1897" *P,* clear 5 3/8" globe *EMB* "NP RR,"
TOB 75.00
"NP RY"—(lid) "Armspear, 1889" *P,* clear 5½" globe,
EMB "NP RY, SAFETY ALWAYS" at rear, *TOB* 85.00
"PE RY"—(lid) "Adams & Westlake Co., Adlake Reliable,
1913" *P,* clear 5 3/8" globe etched "PE RY,
SAFETY FIRST" at rear 65.00
"P RR"—(lid) "Adams & Westlake Co., BB, 1895" *P,* clear
5 3/8" globe *EMB* "P RR 135.00
"P RR"—(lid) "Adams & Westlake Co., Adlake Reliable,
1913" *P,* clear 5 3/8" globe *EMB* Keystone logo 75.00
"P&R RY LOCO DEPT"—(lid) "Armspear, 1889" *P,* clear
5 3/8" globe *EMB* "P&R RY," bracket arm, *TOB* 85.00
"OSL"—(lid) "Adams & Westlake Co., The Adams, 1909"
P, clear 5 3/8" globe *EMB* "OSL" 175.00
ROCK ISLAND"—(logo dome) "Adams & Westlake Co.,
Adlake 250 Kero, 1923" *P,* clear 3¼" globe
unmarked 35.00
"ROCK ISLAND LINES"—(lid) "Adams & Westlake Co.,
Adlake Reliable, 1913" *P,* clear 5 3/8" globe, *EMB*
"ROCK ISLAND LINES" 85.00

Conductor's lanters — brass and nickel plated

"SANTA FE A"—(lid) "Adams & Westlake Co., The
Adams," *BB,* "1909" *P,* clear 5 3/8" globe *EMB*
"SANTA FE," cross logo 195.00
"SOO LINE"—(lid) "Dressel," *NPD,* amber 3¼" globe
unmarked 40.00
"SOO LINE"—(lid) "Armspear, 1895" *P,* red 5 3/8" globe
EMB "SOO LINE," *TOB* 145.00
"SOO LINE"—(lid) "Adams & Westlake Co., Adlake
Reliable, 1913" *P,* clear 5 3/8" globe *EMB* "SOO
LINE, SAFETY ALWAYS" at rear 125.00
"SP CO"—(dome) "Adams & Westlake Co., Adlake 250
Kero, 1923" *P,* clear 3¼" globe unmarked 34.00
"UNION PACIFIC"—(lid) "Adams & Westlake Co., Adlake
Reliable, 1913" *P,* clear 5 3/8" globe unmarked 65.00
UNMARKED—"Adams & Westlake Co., Adlake Reliable,
1913" *P,* clear 5 3/8" globe unmarked 35.00
UNMARKED—"Adams & Westlake Co., Adlake No. 31,"
NPD, battery model 15.00

CONDUCTOR'S HAND LANTERNS

Nickel plated conductor's lanterns and the many varieties of
early brass types are rare and usually go on the auction block.
Examples below are listed alphabetically by manufacturer.

"ADAMS & WESTLAKE CO."—nickel plated, *BB,* globe
half-green, half clear 500.00

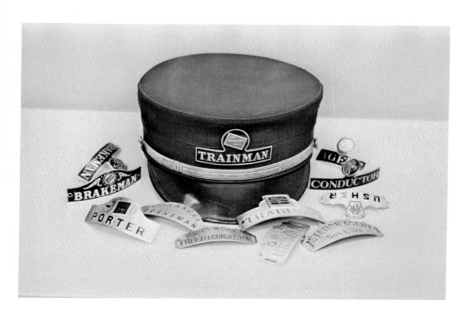

Cap and cap badges

Cap and breast badges

Menus

Passes

Pinbacks

Railroad Brotherhood emblem charms

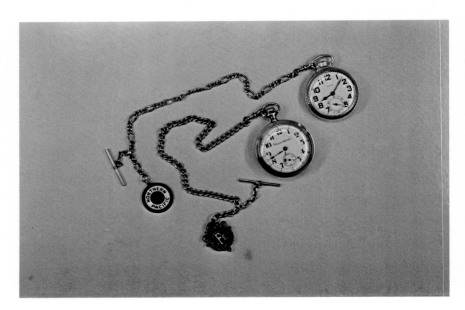

Railroadmen's pocket watches

Switch keys

Conductor's lantern, switch stand lamp, and trainman's lantern

Switch stand lamps

Luggage stickers

Paperweight and pass, 1890s

Timetables, prior to 1900

Playing cards. Grand Trunk Railway, 1900; Chicago & Alton Railway, 1903

Service plate, steam

Service plate, diesel

Pocket mirror, Frisco system

"ADAMS & WESTLAKE CO."—nickel plated, *BB*, globe
half-green, half clear, conductor's name etched in
wreath 700.00
"ADAMS & WESTLAKE CO."—nickel plated, *BB*,
"PULLMAN" on base and etched on clear globe 300.00
"M.M. BUCK & CO."—nickel plated, wire ring bottom,
whale oil burner, early 375.00
"PETER GRAY, BOSTON"—nickel plated, *BB*, clear
globe 250.00
"F.H. LOVELL & CO."—brass, *BB*, whale oil burner,
early 450.00

LOCKS

The earlier switch locks were made of brass, later ones of iron or
steel. The railroad's name or initials were on the shackle or on
the front or back side of the lock. Other letters, numbers,
manufacturer's name and patent dates often appear somewhere
on the lock. The lock is sometimes found with a short length of
iron chain used to fasten it to the switch-stand. The all-brass,
heart-shape switch lock is the most popular and has the higher
value.

The railroads had many other types of locks for general purpose
use. All of these old railroad marked padlocks are being collected today.

SWITCH — (all are brass unless otherwise noted)

"AT&SF RY"—incised on shackle, heart shape,
"UNION BRASS," ca. 1880s 125.00
"BCR&M RR"—incised on shackle, heart shape, "ADRIAN
MICH," ca. 1870s (rare) 185.00
"BURLINGTON"—incised on shackle, steel, brass rivets, no
maker's mark 10.00
"CM&StP RR"—cast on back panel, heart shape,
"LOEFFELHOLZ"....................................55.00
"CM&StP RR"—incised on back, "ADLAKE" on drop, steel,
iron chain, 1923 ....15.00
"CMStP&P RR"—incised on shackle, steel, "Pat. March 5,
1929, FRAIM," chain 18.00
"CMStP&P RR"—incised on shackle, heart shape,
"HANSL MFG." 1956, chain 25.00

"C&NW"—incised on shackle, heart shape, "SLAYMAKER," chain, early 1900s 55.00
"CPR"—raised on key drop, steel, "MITCHELL" 17.50
"CRI&P RR"—incised on shackle, heart shape, "UNION BRASS CO.," ca 1880s 125.00
"CRI&P"—incised on back, "Pat. Mar 20, 1920," steel, "ADLAKE" on drop 20.00
"CStPM&O RY" —incised on shackle, "Pat. Sept. 24, 1912," steel, "ADLAKE" on drop, chain 20.00
"CStPM&O RY"—incised on shackle, heart shape, "SLAYMAKER," chain, early 1900s 65.00
"DL&W"—incised on shackle, heart shape, "FRAIM," chain, early 1900s 45.00
"D&SF"—incised on shackle, heart shape, "EAGLE LOCK CO." (rare) 125.00
"FE&MV"—incised on shackle, heart shape, "Pat. 1879, BOHANNAN" 95.00
"GN RY"—incised on shackle, steel, "SLAYMAKER, Pat. 1915" 18.00
"GN RY"—cast ornate into entire back side, heart shape, "SLAYMAKER," early 1900s 135.00
"MRR CO"—cast on back panel, heart shape, "MILLER LOCK CO.," early 1900s 50.00
"MHC&W RR"—incised on shackle, heart shape, "Pat. June 25, '79, W. BOHANNAN," chain (rare) 135.00
"MK&T—incised on shackle, steel, "SLAYMAKER" on drop, 1948, chain 11.00
"M&StL RY"—incised on shackle, steel, "F.S.HDW." on drop, 1938, chain 25.00

Switch, signal, and general use locks

"NYB&M RR"—incised on back panel, heart shape,
"T. SLAITGH," ca. 1870s 95.00
"NPR"—cast on back panel, heart shape, "FRAIM,"
1911 ....55.00
"NORTHERN PACIFIC"—cast on back panel, "SWITCH"
raised, heart shape, "ADLAKE" on drop 65.00

**Heart shape
switch lock with
fancy initials**

"N&W RY"—cast on entire back side, heart shape, 1952,
no maker's mark 38.00
"PRR CO"—cast ornately on entire back, heart shape,
"FRAIM," 1911 ....95.00
"StPM&M RR"—incised on shackle, heart shape, "UNION
BRASS CO." 1880s. (rare) 150.00
"StP&P RR"—incised on shackle, heart shape, "UNION
BRASS CO." 1870s. (rare) 185.00
"StPSY CO"—incised on shackle, heart shape, "A&W CO."
on drop 35.00
"SOO LINE"—incised on shackle, steel, "ADLAKE"
embossed on drop, no maker's mark, recent 9.00
"SO. RY"—incised on shackle, banjo style with brass rivets,
"YALE," chain 25.00
"UP RR"—cast on back with "SWITCH," heart shape,
1951, chain, no maker's mark 50.00
"UNION PACIFIC"—cast on back panel, "SWITCH CS-1"
raised, heart shape, "ADLAKE," chain 45.00
"UNION PACIFIC"—cast on back panel, "CLOSE THE
LOCK TO GET THE KEY OUT" cast on drop, "A&W CO"
on shackle, chain 48.00

"USY OF O"—incised on back with patent numbers,
"ADLAKE" embossed on drop 18.00

SIGNAL — (all are brass unless otherwise noted)

"AT&SF RY"—incised on bottom edge, "EAGLE
LOCK CO." ca. 1930s 35.00
"B&M RR"—incised on shackle, small heart shape,
"WILSON BOHANNAN" 22.50
"C&A"—incised on shackle with "SIGNAL," small heart
shape, "MILLER" on drop 17.50
"D&H"—incised "THE D&H" on front, "SIGNAL" at bottom
edge, "YALE" 18.00
"DL&W RR"—cast on back panel, "REMOVE KEY WHEN
LOCKING" cast on key drop, "SLAYMAKER" 18.50
"GN RY"—raised on back panel, "REMOVE KEY
WHEN LOCKING" cast on key drop, "SLAY-
MAKER" 18.00
"IC RR"—raised on back panel, small, heart shape,
no maker's mark 10.00
"JERSEY CENTRAL LINES"—incised in circle on front,
signal number on back, no maker's mark 15.00
"NICKEL PLATE RR"—cast in front circle, "SIGNAL
DEPT." incised, "YALE" 20.00
"P&LE RR"—cast in front circle, "SIGNAL DEPT."
incised, "YALE" 24.00
"ROCK ISLAND LINES"—incised on front with "SIGNAL"
below, "CORBIN" with patent numbers on back 12.00
"SOO LINE"—incised on shackle, with "SIGNAL, REMOVE
KEY WHEN LOCKING" cast on drop, small heart
shape, 1930s, no maker's mark 35.00
"SOUTHERN RY"—cast on back panel with "SIGNAL,"
large heart shape, "A&W CO." on key drop 45.00
"UP RR"—incised on front, with "CS-61 SIGNAL USE NO
OIL," small, chain, no maker's mark 15.00
"WABASH"—flag emblem cast in circle, "SIGNAL
DEPT." incised, "YALE" 25.00

MISCELLANEOUS

"B&O RR"—incised on front, small steel, brass rivets,
shanty, no maker 15.00

"CB&Q RR"—incised on back, steel, brass rivets,
"CORBIN," general use 18.00
"CB&Q RR"—raised on drop, small steel, shanty, no
maker's mark 12.00
"FRISCO"—cast on front, "DON'T USE OIL BUT
PLENTY OF GRAPHITE" on back, brass, "KEEN
CUTTER," general use 75.00
"GN RY"—incised on shackle, steel, shield shape,
"MILLER LOCK CO." 1920s, general use 25.00
"M&StL RR"—incised on front shackle, "ROAD DEPT."
on rear shackle, brass, small heart shape,
"FRAIM" 60.00
"M&StL RR"—incised on shackle, steel, heart shape,
"F-S HDW CO." shanty 35.00
"MStP&SSM"—incised on shackle, brass, heart shape,
"SHOREHAM SHOPS" on drop, "F-S HDW. 1932" on
back side 50.00
"RY.EX.AGY."—incised on shackle and back side, steel,
"Pat. 11-21-05," general use, no maker's mark 30.00
"SOUTHERN PACIFIC"—Sunset logo cast on front, brass
heart shape, early 1900s, general use, no maker's
mark 45.00
"UNION PACIFIC"—with "CS-21 ROADWAY & BRIDGE
DEPARTMENT" cast on entire back, brass, heart
shape, "ADLAKE," chain 40.00

LOCOMOTIVE BUILDER'S PLATES

Locomotives have always been identified with the name of their
builders by means of a metal plaque usually affixed on each side

Diesel locomotive builder's plate

of the smokebox. They were made in various shapes and sizes with the name of the locomotive company, serial number, location of the works, and year date of completion. Builder's plates from the steam era are much in demand and have become scarce and valuable. Examples of plates from the more common producers are listed here. Reproductions have come on the market, so be wary.

AMERICAN—"American Locomotive Company," Serial No., "Schenectady Works, July, 1912," brass rectangle with rounded corners, 7½" x 14" 150.00

AMERICAN—"American Locomotive Co., General Electric Co., Schenectady, N.Y.," Serial No., "November, 1948," Alco-GE trademarks, cast iron rectangle, 6" x 12", diesel 50.00

BALDWIN—"Built By The Baldwin Locomotive Works, Philadelphia, Pa.," Serial No., "August, 1913," bronze rectangle, 3½" x 9" 125.00

BALDWIN—"The Baldwin Locomotive Works," Serial No., "Philadelphia, U.S.A., August, 1914," bronze disc, 9¼" diameter 200.00

BALDWIN—"Baldwin Locomotive Works, Philadelphia, U.S.A., Burnham Williams & Co.," Serial No., "August, 1905," brass disc, 16½" diameter 300.00

LIMA—"Lima Locomotive Works, Incorporated, December, 1939," brass, diamond shape, 9" x 15" 175.00

GM—"General Motors Locomotives, EMD, Electric-Motive Division," Serial No., year date, embossed sheet metal enameled with red and blue colors, elongated oval shape, 4½" x 15", diesel 35.00

PORTER—"H.K. Porter Company, Pittsburgh, U.S.A.," Serial No., brass, shield shape, 8" x 8" 150.00

Steam locomotive builder's plate

LUGGAGE STICKERS

During the Golden Years of the passenger train, when travel by train was the way to go, colorful paper labels with a gummed back were handed out at the ticket counters to be pasted on suitcases and valises. It was a common sight to see these stickers on luggage everywhere, toted by tourists advertising that they were riding the popular "name trains" and had been or were going to the many vacation spots throughout the country. These unused luggage stickers are now being sought after. Those from the steam era are harder to find and worth more than those issued during the waning years of rail travel.

"BURLINGTON ROUTE"—Cut-out profile of Buffalo Bill with slogan, "Yellowstone Park via Cody Road" 15.00

"BURLINGTON ROUTE"—Round sticker, aluminum foil type in blue, depicting the silver ZEPHYR at center 5.00

"C&O"—Round sticker showing sleepy kitten within a heart entitled "THE GEORGE WASHINGTON," "Sleep like a Kitten" 5.00

"C&NW"—Small square sticker with slogan, "The Famous 400" "6½ hrs. Chicago-Twin Cities, 409 miles— 390 minutes" 4.50

Luggage stickers

"CHICAGO & NORTHWESTERN-UNION PACIFIC"— Hexagon style sticker showing the yellow streamliner, CITY OF DENVER, and slogan, "World's Fastest Long Distance Train" 10.00

"GN RY"—Large round sticker, mountain goat atop logo encircled with slogan, "See America First, Glacier National Park" 18.00

"MILWAUKEE ROAD"—Round sticker depicting HIAWATHA steam train No. 1 at center, with slogan, "Nothing Faster On Rails" below 7.50

"MILWAUKEE ROAD"—Round sticker depicting the electric train, "OLYMPIAN," in black, purple and orange colors 8.00

"MO-PAC"—Cut-out sticker of black steam engine with red buzz-saw logo entitled "THE SUNSHINE SPECIAL" with ad copy below 12.50

"MO-PAC"—Cut-out sticker of black steam engine and red buzz-saw logo entitled "THE SCENIC LIMITED" with ad copy below 12.50

"MO-PAC"—Large red and white buzz-saw logo 3.50

"NORTHWESTERN-UNION PACIFIC"—Round label type sticker with wavy border entitled "The Streamliner CITY OF DENVER." 3.00

"NORTHWESTERN-UNION PACIFIC"—Round label type sticker with wavy border entitled "The Streamliner CITY OF LOS ANGELES." 3.00

"PRR". Burgundy red keystone logo entitled "Travel By Train" 3.50

"SANTA FE"—Square type, blue and silver, with Indian and logo at center, entitled "SUPER CHIEF" 3.50

"SANTA FE"—Round sticker, red logo on yellow at upper right, entitled "EL CAPITAN" 2.50

"SP"—Round logo, "SOUTHERN PACIFIC LINES" in blue, white and gold 3.50

"SP"—Large square label type with streamlined "DAYLIGHT" engine depicted in white, orange and black on yellow 4.00

MAGAZINES

Literally thousands of railroad magazines were published down through the years for both the trainman and the general public. Many were put out by the Brotherhood for the engineer, fireman, carman, and other members. Also the railroads themselves published various inter-company magazines for their employees. Railroad magazines for the public, both pulp and slick paper, have been in publication from the turn of the century up to the present time.

A series of dime novels, published weekly for the American youth, was issued around the turn of the century, with names such as *Pluck And Luck, Work And Win, Brave And Bold,* to name a few. These early pulps had eye-catching front covers with illustrations of exciting railroad scenes, and are being picked up too. Copies of all these various magazines in fine condition are bringing good prices today.

BROTHERHOOD

LOCOMOTIVE ENGINEER'S JOURNAL—September,
1920 ....3.50
LOCOMOTIVE ENGINEER'S JOURNAL—March,
1940 ....2.00
LOCOMOTIVE FIREMAN'S MAGAZINE—June,
1905 ....5.00
*LOCOMOTIVE FIREMEN AND ENGINEMEN'S
MAGAZINE*—October, 1911 ....4.00
RAILWAY AGE AND SERVICE MAGAZINE—March,
1882 ....10.00
RAILWAY CARMEN'S JOURNAL—May, 1908 ....5.00
RAILROAD TRAINMEN'S JOURNAL—February,
1894 ....8.00
RAILROAD TRAINMEN'S JOURNAL—May, 1903 ....5.00
THE RAILROAD TRAINMAN—January, 1940 ....2.00

INTER-COMPANY

MAINE-CENTRAL RAILROAD EMPLOYEES MAGAZINE,
Vol. 3, No's 1-12 Oct. 1946-Sept. 1947, complete
set 10.00
NORTHWESTERN RAILWAY MAGAZINE—C&NW RR—
October, 1923 ....4.00
ROCK ISLAND MAGAZINE—CRI&P— RR—October, 1922,
70th Anniv. Number 15.00
THE FOUR TRACK NEWS—NYC&HR RR, April,
1903 ....5.00
THE MILWAUKEE ROAD MAGAZINE—CMStP&P RR—
July/Aug. 1957 ....1.50

PUBLIC

MODERN RAILROAD—March, 1955 ....1.00
RAILROAD MAN'S MAGAZINE (pulp) March 1939 ....2.50
RAILROAD STORIES (pulp)—May, 1932 ....3.50

BOY'S WEEKLYS

Boy's weekly magazines

Railroadmen's and public magazines

MAPS

Roll-down maps issued by the railroads were used in classrooms and libraries. Large system maps hung on the walls of railroad ticket offices and depots. Tourist guide maps were handed out freely by the railroads. Private firms also published railroad maps for the public's use. There are also railroad commissioner's state maps and a wide array of other old railroad maps issued

Wall map

down through the years. The early rare maps bring the higher prices.

BURLINGTON ROUTE—Vacation folder map, 19" x 37",
Yellowstone Park, 1938 ....5.00
CRAM'S—Railroad pocket map, Wisconsin, unfolds
19" x 24", soft cover, 1885 ....25.00

Miscellaneous railroad maps

GOLDTHWAIT'S—Railroad map, New England States,
Canada, Eastern New York, unfolds 18" x 24", hard
cover, 1850. (rare) 50.00
GN RY—Topographic map of Glacier National Park,
Montana, unfolds 31" x 34", cloth backed, hard
cover, 1922 ....20.00
M&S RR—framed wall map, 23" x 39", lines and con-
nections, 1856 (rare) 75.00
MO-PAC—World map, 38" x 51", classroom type, rolling
rods, 1950 ....25.00
NP—Mounted wall map, 23" x 35", line and connections,
1893 ....35.00
ROCK ISLAND—travel folder map, 18" x 32", U.S. and
System, 1924 ....7.50
SP—U.S. map, 41" x 51", wall, roller type, 1951 ....25.00
UP—Tourist folding map, 18" x 32", U.S. and System,
1922 ....8.50
R.R. COMMISSIONER—Map of Minnesota, 31" x 50",
folding pocket type, 1925 ....6.00
R.R. COMMISSIONER—Map of Montana, unfolds
40" x 53", cloth backed, hard cover, 1908 ....25.00

116

MEDALLIONS AND MEDALS

Railroads issued many medallions and medals down through the years commemorating special events in their history, their anniversaries, and also for safety efforts. Most were made of brass of bronze in various diameters, occasionally rectangular in shape, depicting locomotives and historical events. Medals were also issued to railroads for their safety efforts and prevention of accidents. Prices are based on the rarity of the medallion or medal.

B&O—1827-1927 100th Anniversary medallion, bronze, 2¾" diameter, Tom Thumb and modern passenger train, obverse and reverse 85.00

C&NW—Safety Award medallion, bronze, 2¾" diameter, E.H. Harriman profile on obverse, trainman walking track on reverse 50.00

Centennial medallion

D&H—1827-1927 100th Anniversary medallion, bronze, rectangular, 2½" x 4", commemorating the Stourbridge Lion's first successful trip, Aug. 8, 1829, at Honesdale, Pa. 100.00

GN RY—Memorial medallion, 1916, bronze, 3" diameter, James J. Hill profile obverse, wreath and year dates reverse 18.00

IC—1851-1951 100 year Centennial medallion, bronze, 3" diameter, diamond logo and map, obverse and reverse 35.00

117

IC—1851-1951 100 year Centennial medal, bronze, smaller
size 1 3/8", identical to the larger issue 15.00

Anniversary medal — obverse and reverse

SANTA FE—1868-1968-2068, Second Century Progress
medal, brass, 1½" diameter, logo and progress, obverse
and reverse 10.00
UP—1869-1969 Centennial Celebration medallion, bronze,
2½" diameter, golden spike obverse, two locomotives
reverse 20.00
UP—1869-1969 Centennial Celebration medal, bronze,
smaller size, 1¼", identical to the larger issue 10.00

PASSES

Passes were issued by the railroads down through the years to officials of railroads, newspapermen, politicians, clergymen, and other favored persons. Passes from the 1850s and 1860s bring top prices. Passes with locomotives, trains, picturesque scenes and ornate designs on them are highly desirable and priced according to their pictorial or historical significance, as are those from obscure, short lived and now defunct roads. Passes from the 1940s up to the present time have lower value.

Railroads also issued passes to their employees and their families. These were either annual passes or were good for one trip only. They were usually made of card stock, but a great many were made of paper stock, larger than the standard size pass. Employee passes are generally priced lower, exceptions being the uncommon and long gone railroads.

There were also passes issued by express companies, telegraph companies, omnibus lines, the Pullman Company, etc. in connection with the railroads, allowing the holder to occupy a Pullman seat or berth, to transport packages, to send telegrams, to cross a river on a toll bridge or ferryboat, to get transporation between depots and hotels, and so on, without charge. Value on these various railroad-related passes are based according to their rarity.

PUBLIC

"ALABAMA CENTRAL RAILROAD"—1876 . . . . .15.00
"ALLEGHENY VALLEY RAILROAD"—1873,
  locomotive 16.50
"ATLANTIC, MISSISSIPPI & OHIO R.R."—1873,
  ornate engraving 18.50
"ATLANTIC & PACIFIC R.R."—1873, Eads bridge, St.
  Louis 17.50
"AVON, GENESEO & MT. MORRIS RR."— 1868 . . . . .20.00
"BALTIMORE & OHIO R.R."—1873, train 16.50
"BUFFALO, ROCHESTER & PITTSBURGH"—
  1894 . . . . .8.00
"BURLINGTON & LAMOILLE RR."—1884 . . . . .10.00
"BURLINGTON, CEDAR RAPIDS & NORTHERN
  RY."—1900 . . . . .7.50
"CHESAPEAKE & OHIO R.R."—1930 . . . . .3.00
"CHESHIRE & ASHEULUT RR."—1873 . . . . .10.00
"CHICAGO & ALTON R.R."—1865, eagles and flags 25.00

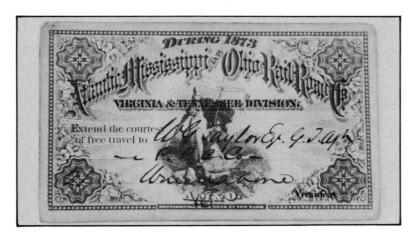

Ornate annual pass

"CHICAGO & ALTON R.R."—1895, full length
passenger train 12.00
"CHICAGO & ALTON R.R."—1896, Father Time in
locomotive cab, colored lithograph 13.50
"CHICAGO GREAT WESTERN RY."—1898, colorful
maple leaf emblem 10.00
"CHICAGO, MILWAUKEE & ST. PAUL RY."—
1875 . . . . 15.00

Pass picturing locomotive

"CHICAGO & NORTHWESTERN RY."—1897 . . . . 8.50
"CHICAGO & ROCK ISLAND R.R."—1865, train
on bridge and steamboat 27.50
"CHICAGO, ST. PAUL & KANSAS CITY RY."— 1891,
clergyman's 1/2 fare permit. 10.00
"CHICAGO, ST. PAUL, MPLS. & OMAHA RY."—
1912 . . . . 5.00
"CHICAGO, SOUTH SHORE & SOUTH BEND"—
1963-1964 . . . . 1.00
"CORNING, COWANESQUE & ANTRIM RY."—1876,
picturesque 15.00
"DAYTON & UNION R.R."—1868, ornate 20.00
"DELAWARE, LACKAWANNA & WESTERN RR."—
1869 . . . . 10.00
"DULUTH SOUTH SHORE & ATLANTIC RY."—
1891, picturesque harbor scene 12.50
"ELGIN, JOLIET & EASTERN RY."—1895 . . . . 8.00
"ERIE RAILWAY"—1874, picturesque 16.00
"EVANSVILLE & TERRE HAUTE R.R."—1897 . . . . 6.00
"FLINT & PERE MARQUETTE RY."—1873, train on
covered bridge 16.50
"FLORIDA CENTRAL & PENINSULAR R.R."—1896 . . . . . . 6.00
"FLORIDA EAST COAST RY."—1899 . . . . 6.00

"GEORGIA, SOUTHERN & FLORIDA RY."—1899 . . . . . . .6.00

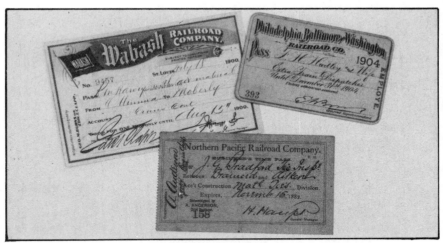

Employee passes

"GREAT NORTHERN RY."—1911 . . . . .5.25
"GREAT WESTERN RY. OF CANADA"—1865,
train on suspension bridge 25.00
"GULF & SHIP ISLAND R.R."—1898 . . . . .7.00
"ILLINOIS CENTRAL R.R."—1865, picturesque depot
scene 25.00
"INDIANA, DECATUR & WESTERN RY."—1896 . . . . .7.00
"INTERNATIONAL & GREAT NORTHERN RR."—1899,
American & Mexican flags 10.00
"IOWA CENTRAL RY."—1898, farming & industry
scene 10.00
"JACKSONVILLE, LOUISVILLE & ST. LOUIS"—1895 . . . .6.00
"KANSAS PACIFIC RY."—1873 . . . . .10.00
"KANSAS CITY SOUTHERN"—1909 . . . . .5.00
"LACROSSE & MILWAUKEE R.R."—1863 . . . . .15.00
"LAKE ERIE & WESTERN RY."—1882, editor's pass,
photo of bearer (rare) 30.00
"LAKE SHORE & MICHIGAN SOUTHERN RY."—
1895 . . . . .7.00
"LOUISVILLE, CINCINNATI & LEXINGTON R.R.,"
Shortline—1873, train on bridge 15.00
"MANISTEE & NORTHWESTERN R.R."—1896, train and
lake steamer 10.00
"MANITOBA & NORTHWESTERN RY. OF CANADA"—
1895, locomotive 11.00

"MICHIGAN CENTRAL R.R."—1865, Great Central Union
Depot 25.00
"MPLS. & ST.LOUIS RY."—1944-45 . . . . .2.00
"MPLS. ST.PAUL& SAULT STE. MARIE RY."—1917 . . . . . .4.50
"MISSOURI PACIFIC R.R."—1920 . . . . .4.00
"MOBILE & BIRMINGHAM R.R."—1897, passenger
train 10.00
"NEW YORK CENTRAL"—1953-1954 . . . . .1.25
"NEW YORK, PENNSYLVANIA & OHIO R.R."—
1883, clergyman's certificate 12.00
"NORTH MISSOURI R.R."—1865, 4-4-0 locomotive 25.00
"NORTHERN PACIFIC R.R."—1880 . . . . .13.00
"OGDENSBURG & LAKE CHAMPLAIN R.R."—
1870 . . . . .12.00
"OHIO RIVER R.R."—1895, locomotive 10.00
"OHIO VALLEY R.R."—1896 . . . . .6.00
"OIL CREEK & ALLEGHENY RIVER RY."—1873,
oil well derrick 16.50
"PENNSYLVANIA RAILROAD"—1868, editorial 20.00
"PENNSYLVANIA RAILROAD"—1873, horses 18.00
"PENNSYLVANIA RAILROAD"—1948 . . . . .1.50
"PERE MARQUETTE R.R."—1902 . . . . .5.00
"PITTSBURGH & CONNELSVILLE R.R."—1870 . . . . .18.00
"PLANT SYSTEM RYS."—1897 . . . . .7.00
"QUEEN & CRESCENT ROUTE"—1895 . . . . .6.00
"QUINCY, ALTON & ST. LOUIS R.R."—1873 . . . . .10.00
"RALEIGH & WESTERN RY."—1895 . . . . .6.00

"ROCK ISLAND & PEORIA RY."—1895, train 10.00
"ROME, WATERTOWN & OGDENSBURGH R.R."—
1868 . . . . .15.00
"ST. LOUIS & IRON MOUNTAIN R.R."—1865,
primitive train 25.00
"ST. LOUIS & SAN FRANCISCO RY."—1881,
locomotive engraving 14.50
"ST. PAUL & DULUTH R.R."—1892, engraved
scenes 10.50
"ST. PAUL, MPLS. & MANITOBA RY."—1881, Jas. J.
Hill signature 35.00
"ST. PAUL & PACIFIC R.R.," First Division—
1866 . . . . .22.50
"ST. PAUL & PACIFIC R.R."—1877 . . . . .14.50
"SOUTHERN MINNESOTA R.R."—1879 . . . . .13.50
"SOUTHERN PACIFIC"—1946-1948 . . . . .1.50
"TALLASSEE & MONTGOMERY RY."—1896 . . . . .6.00
"TAURES & GULF R.R."—1895, train 10.00
"TOLEDO, PEORIA & WARSAW RY."—1869 . . . . .15.00

"UTAH CENTRAL R.R."—1876 . . . . .15.00
"VERMONT CENTRAL & VT. & CANADA R.ROADS"—
  1870, depot scene 18.00
"WABASH, ST.LOUIS & PACIFIC RY."—1886 . . . . .11.75
"WESTERN UNION R.R."—1869 .10.00
"WISCONSIN CENTRAL LINES"—1889, train on
  bridge 12.50
"YAZOO & MISSISSIPPI VALLEY R.R."—1898 . . . . .6.00

EMPLOYEE

"CHICAGO, MILWAUKEE & ST. PAUL RY."—1887,
  annual 9.50
"CHICAGO & NORTHWESTERN RY."—1884, trip 10.00
"COLORADO MIDLAND"—1916, annual 15.00
"DULUTH & IRON RANGE R.R."—1892, trip 9.00
"GREAT NORTHERN RY."—1901, time 6.50
"GREEN BAY, WINONA & ST.PAUL R.R."—1889,
  trip 9.50
"HOCKING VALLEY RY."—1908, time 5.50
"ILLINOIS CENTRAL R.R."—1892, trip 8.50
"MICHIGAN CENTRAL R.R."—1894, trip 8.00
"MPLS. & ST.LOUIS R.R."—1930, annual 3.00
"MISSOURI PACIFIC RY."—1899, trip 7.50
"NORTHERN PACIFIC R.R."—1904, exchange trip 6.00

Miscellaneous passes — express, telegraph, etc.

"PHILADELPHIA, WILMINGTON & BALTIMORE
R.R."—1899, annual 7.50
"SOUTHERN RAILWAY"—1914, annual 4.00
"TOLEDO, CINCINNATI & ST.LOUIS R.R."—1883,
trip 9.50
"WABASH RAILROAD"—1900, trip 7.00
"WISCONSIN CENTRAL LINES"—1892, trip 8.50

MISCELLANEOUS

"ADAMS EXPRESS COMPANY"—1895 .... 9.00
"AMERICAN EXPRESS COMPANY"—1896,
watchdog 8.75
"ILLINOIS & ST.LOUIS BRIDGE"—1876, bridge and
river scene 15.00
"NATIONAL EXPRESS COMPANY"—1902 .... 6.75
"NATIONAL MAIL COMPANY"—1895, stagecoach 12.00
"PARMELEE CO. CHICAGO OMNIBUS LINE"—
1903 .... 6.50
"POSTAL TELEGRAPH-CABLE COMPANY"—
1902 .... 6.75
"PULLMAN'S PALACE CAR COMPANY"—1873,
Geo. M. Pullman signature 25.00
"SENECA LAKE STEAM NAVIGATION CO."—1895,
steamboat and train 15.00
"UNITED STATES EXPRESS COMPANY"—1899,
horseshoe trademark 8.75
"WESTERN EXPRESS COMPANY"—1900 .... 7.50
"WESTERN UNION TELEGRAPH COMPANY"—1873 .... 16.00
"WIGGINS FERRY COMPANY"—1876 .... 18.00
"WOODRUFF SLEEPING & PARLOR COACH CO."—
1873, Jonah Woodruff signature 25.00

PINBACKS

Thousands of pinbacks were worn by railroad employees and also handed out freely by the railroads to the general public. They carried safety slogans, promotional advertising, named passenger trains, etc. Some have a history dating back to the turn of the century. There are many collectors for these colorful old celluloid pinback buttons, and they are getting scarce, with prices on the increase.

Celluloid pinback buttons

AMTRAK—"Tracks Are Back!" black letters on white, 2 1/8" diameter 3.00

AMTRAK—1973, "Ride The Turbo!" white on aqua, 1¾" diameter 2.00

ACL—100% Safety, 1931, white on purple. 7/8" diameter 6.00

BCR&N RY —Red diamond logo on white, 7/8" diameter 20.00

BN—1967, "Safety-Courtesy-Dependability," white goat on blue, 1¼" diameter 2.50

BN—1969, "Pace Your Life To Live," white goat on gold, 1¼" diameter 2.00

BURLINGTON ROUTE—Logo, tracks, 1850-1940, white background, 11/16" diameter 3.00

BURLINGTON ROUTE—Silver Zephyr on dark blue, 1¼" diameter 5.00

CPR—Beaver atop red shield logo. "Get Your Canadian Home From The Canadian Pacific," black on white, 1" diameter 15.00

C&O RY—Chessie kitten on white background, 1½" diameter 12.00

CC&L—"The Straight Line," black and red on white, ¾" diameter 5.00

CM&StP RY—red logo, "Safety First" on white, 1" diameter 6.00

CM&StP RY—"Opportunity, Orchard Homes, Government Homesteads," red logo on white and yellow, 1½" diameter 20.00

C&NW LINE—Black and red logo and "Passenger Agent," on white, 2¼" diameter 8.00

GN RY—Rectangle logo, American flag, house, "Free Homes In Central Oregon" on dark blue, 1¾" diameter 18.00

GN RY—Goat atop logo, "See America First: Glacier National Park," red on yellow, 1½" diameter 12.50

GN RY—Logo, "P.P.I.E., 1915," blue and gold on grey with attached blue and gold ribbons, 1¾" diameter 20.00

GN RY—Logo at center with red, white and blue circles, 1½" diameter 10.00

GN RY—Goat atop streamline diesel train, "The Red River, 1950" orange, green and white, 1¾" diameter 15.00

GN RY—Goat, "1953 Safety Campaign," red and black on white, 1¼" diameter 4.00

GN RY—Goat, "Century Of Safety And Progress, 1862-1962," blue and gold on white, 1¾" diameter 3.50

GN RY—Goat in diesel cab, "You're On The Right Track With Great Northern," yellow background, 2¼" diameter 6.00

LV RR—Red flag logo with wreath, "Black Diamond Express," white background, 7/8" diameter 12.50

MILWAUKEE ROAD—Red logo, "Chicago Railroad Fair, No. 24348," black on white, 1¾" diameter 8.00

MILWAUKEE ROAD—Indian figure, "Hiawatha Tribe Member," black on yellow, 1¼" diameter 4.00

NORTHWESTERN LINE—Logo at center with "Alfalfa, The Great Wealth Producer," black on dull yellow, 1¼" diameter 10.00

NP—"Yellowstone Park Line" logo, red and black on white, 1¾" diameter 10.00

NP—"Yellowstone Park Line" logo, red and black on white, 1¼" diameter 5.00

UP—Shield logo, "Union Pacific Family," "Service,"
"War Club," on red background, 7/8" diameter 7.50
UP—"Employee Booster's League," white and red on dark
blue, oval, 5/8" x 1" 5.00

PLAYING CARDS

Railroad playing cards go back to around the turn of the century.
The earlier souvenir packs had pictoral scenes on their faces and
usually came in a two-piece cardboard slipcase. Subsequent
decks with regular face cards came in a standard cardstock case
with a folding end flap. Packs most in demand and having the
higher value are those from the early 1900s, especially decks
featuring steam trains, colorful advertising, and interesting logo
designs on their backs. Decks with missing or damaged cards,
and not in their original box or case, must be discounted in
price.

AMTRAK—Logo on backs, original case, recent 3.00
ACL—Diesel locomotive 525 and palm trees on backs,
original case 6.00
B&O—"Capitol Ltd." on backs, original slipcase box,
ca. 1926, mint 45.00
B&O—"National Ltd." on backs, original slipcase box,
ca. 1926, mint 45.00
BAR—Logo against red, white and blue bars on backs,
original case 4.00
BURLINGTON ROUTE—"Parade of Progress" on backs,
no case, recent 3.50
BURLINGTON ROUTE—streamlined Zephyr, "America's
distinctive trains" on backs, original 2-piece box,
ca. 1943 .... 11.00

Playing cards — souvenir packs

C&O—C&O, FFV, "East-West via Washington" on backs,
52 scenes on faces, original slipcase box, ca. 1890 . . . . . 75.00
C&A—Red cowboy girl on backs, original case, 1903 . . . . 55.00
CGW—Gold/black logo on red on backs, original case,
ca. 1950 . . . . 12.00
C&NW—Logo on back, classical figure on wheel, original
case, ca. 1935 . . . . 25.00
C&NW—Diesel streamliner across "400" on backs,
original 2-piece box, ca. 1942 . . . . 16.00
C&NW—Yellow diesel locomotive on backs, original 2-piece
box, ca. 1948 . . . . 12.50
CM&StP—Souvenir. Snowcap mtn & pines on backs, 52
scenes on faces, original slipcase box, ca. 1925 . . . . 28.50
CMStP&P—Souvenir. Electric locomotive on backs, 52 scenes
on faces, original slipcase box, ca. 1930 . . . . 28.50
CMStP&P—"The Olympian" electric, on backs, original
2-piece box, ca. 1940 . . . . 18.00
CMStP&P—"Hiawatha #1" on backs, original 2-piece
box, ca. 1942 . . . . 16.00
CMStP&P—Hiawatha figure on backs, original case,
ca. 1965 . . . . 10.00
CO&G—Indian chief on backs, original 2-piece slipcase,
ca. 1899 . . . . 75.00

Playing cards — standard packs

D&RG—Souvenir. Train in Royal Gorge on backs, State
seal in corners, 52 scenes on faces, original slipcase
box, ca 1922 ....38.50
D&RGW—Souvenir. Train in Royal Gorge, suspension
bridge on backs, 52 scenes on faces, original slipcase
box, ca. 1930s 28.50
DM&I—Logo on backs, Armed Forces insignia, original
2-piece box, 1943 ....22.50
GTR—Souvenir. Bonnet girl and roses on backs, 52
scenes on faces, original slipcase box, ca. 1900 ....60.00
GN—Red, white goat logo on backs, original case,
ca. 1930 ....27.50
GN—Blue, mountain goat on backs, black logo at feet,
ca. 1920 ....32.00
GN—Chief Wades-In-The-Water on backs, original case,
ca. 1947 ....12.50
GN—Double deck. Chief Wades-In-The-Water, Julia-
Wades-In-The-Water on backs, original 2 piece box,
ca. 1948. Mint 20.00
GN—Double deck. Chief Middle Rider, Buckskin Pinto
Woman on backs, original slipcase box, ca. 1951.
Mint 20.00
IC—"Panama Ltd." on backs, original case, ca. 1935.
Mint 42.50
IC—"Floridan Ltd." on backs, original case, ca. 1935.
Mint 42.50
IC—Church spires scene on backs, original case,
ca. 1968 ....7.50
L&N—"General" and modern diesel on backs, cellophane
wrapped, recent 5.00
MO-PAC—Double deck. Streamliner Eagle against
mountain background on backs, 2-piece box, 1950s 35.00
MO-PAC—"The Sunshine Special" on backs, original
case, ca. 1926 ....45.00
MO-PAC—Double deck. Buzzsaw logo on backs, original
slipcase, ca. 1932 ....36.00
NYC—"20th Century Ltd., Morning on the Mohawk" on
backs, original box, ca. 1926 ....45.00
NICKEL PLATE ROAD—Silver logo on backs, no box or
case, ca. 1940s 8.50
NP—double Yellowstone Park Line logo on backs, original
case, ca. 1925 ....27.50
NP—Red, single Yellowstone Park Line logo on backs,
original 2-piece slipcase, ca. 1932 ....25.00
NP—Red single monad logo on backs, original case,
ca. 1957 ....10.00

PRR—Centennial. Locomotives, 1846-1946 on backs,
original case 18.00
PRR—Liberty Limited on stone arch-bridge on backs,
2-piece slipcase, ca. 1920s 30.00
PRR—Double deck. Keystone logo on backs, 2-piece box,
ca. 1960s 15.00
ROCK ISLAND—Blue filigree design on backs, double logo,
original case, ca. 1912 . . . . 45.00
ROCK ISLAND—Stylized diesel locomotive design on
backs, original case, recent 5.00
ROCK ISLAND—Double deck. Black, red logo, "Route Of
The Rockets" on backs, original 2-piece box, ca.
1951 . . . . 25.00
SANTA FE—Double deck. Diesel trains on backs, original
plastic box, recent 10.00
SANTA FE—Diesel locomotive #5695 on backs, cello
wrapped, recent 3.50
SOO LINE—Green, gold logo on backs, original case,
ca. 1938 . . . . 27.50
SOO LINE—Double deck. Duluth, Aerial bridge on backs,
original 2-piece box, 1956 . . . . 25.00
SP—Souvenir. Mt. Shasta on backs, 52 scenes on
faces, original 2-piece slipcase, ca. 1915 . . . . 47.50
SP—Souvenir. Train crossing Great Salt Lake on backs,
scenes on faces, original 2-piece slipcase, ca. 1926 . . . . 35.00
SP—Souvenir. Streamliner "Daylight" passing mission
on backs, 52 scenes on faces, original 2-piece slipcase,
ca. 1943 . . . . 25.00
UP—Centennial 1869-1969. Driving Golden Spike on backs,
original case 8.00
UP—Jackson Lake, Teton Range, Wyo. on backs, original
case, ca. 1970 . . . . 5.00
UP—Diesel passenger train on backs, original case, ca.
1971 . . . . 5.00
WP&Y—Souvenir. Blue logo, train on bridge on backs,
52 scenes on faces, original 2-piece slipcase, ca.
1895 . . . . 65.00

POSTCARDS, STEREO VIEW CARDS

Collecting railroad postcards has become very popular in recent years, and interest in them continues to rise. Many collect them by categories, such as locomotives, passenger trains, train wrecks, depots, bridges, or various railroad scenes. Besides those put out by the railroads themselves, thousands were made by various card manufacturers both here and abroad. In addition to the single postcard, folders and booklets of postcards were issued. Pricing depends on the popularity of the category and the physical condition of the cards. Named trains from the steam era are high on the collector's list. Stereoscopic view cards are also included in this category.

Railroad advertising postcards

POSTCARDS

AT&SF—view of shops, Topeka, Kansas. Unused 3.00
B&O—Locomotive No. 5320, "President Cleveland,"
  exhibited at Century Of Progress, Chicago, 1933.
  Postmarked 1933 ....4.00
B&O—"1927 Fair Of The Iron Horse," Halethorpe,
  Maryland. Set of 15 cards, mint 25.00
BURLINGTON ROUTE—Thousand Island Dressing recipe.
  View of dining car interior and recipe ingredients
  listed below. Unused 3.00
C&O—Wreck of passenger train No. 3 near Hinton, West
  Virginia, March 12, 1907 ....9.50

131

C&NW—Interior view of an ultra-modern parlor car on the new streamliner "400." Unused 2.50

CGW—Interior view of a standard steel sleeping car. Unused 2.50

CGW—Repair shops, Oelwein, Iowa. Postmarked 1910 .... 4.00

CM&StP—View of The Overland Limited passenger train, private mailing card. Postmarked 1905 .... 15.00

CM&StP—Depot, Aberdeen, South Dakota. Postmarked 1909 .... 3.50

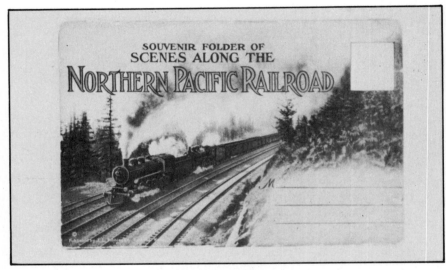

Souvenir folder

CM&StP—Souvenir folder of scenes along the route from Butte, Montana to Puget Sound. Unused 8.00

D&RG—Souvenir folder of scenes over Soldiers Summit, Utah to Salt Lake City, Utah. Unused 8.00

D&SL—Looping the loop of the Continental Divide, Colorado, "Moffat Road." Unused 5.00

ERIE—View of Erie Railroad Yards, Hornell, New York. Postmarked 1910 .... 3.00

GN—Depot scene at Devils Lake, North Dakota. Postmarked 1909 .... 3.50

GN—View of Lake McDonald, Montana. Postmarked 1910 .... 2.00

GN—Souvenir folder of scenes from the Oriental Ltd. enroute St. Paul, Minnesota to Seattle, Washington. Dated 1906 .... 10.00

IC—Streamliner, Panama Ltd., against Michigan Avenue skyline, Chicago. Mint. 4.00

LV—The Black Diamond Express between New York, Philadelphia and Buffalo. Mint 7.50

L&N—Railroad bridge across Ohio river between Evansville, Indiana and Henderson, Kentucky 1952 .... 2.00

MC—view of Miagara Falls from Michigan Central Train. Mint 7.50

NYC—New York Central's "Empire State Express," the fastest long distance train in the world. Embossed card. Postmarked 1908 .... 10.00

NP—A candy train. Model of the North Coast Limited made entirely of sugar, courtesy the dining car bake shop. Mint 5.00

NP—Diesel locomotive 6000 against mountain background. Mint 1.50

NP—Souvenir folder of scenes along their western route to Spokane, Washington. Ca. 1926. Unused 8.00

PRR—Broadway Limited speeding on stone arch bridge, entitled "Speedy and Security." Postmarked 1926 ...... 3.50

ROCK ISLAND—Rocky Mountain Rocket at the foot of famous Pikes Peak. Mint 3.00

ROCK ISLAND—Train wreck at Gowrie, Iowa, Aug. 15, 1910. Postmarked 8.00

SEABOARD—Silver Meteors pass in the scenic highlands of Florida. Mint 3.00

Stereo view card

133

SOO LINE—A modern railway, view of passenger train
Twin Cities to Winnipeg, fifteen hours. Postmarked
1906 . . . . .8.00
SP—Souvenir folder, The Shasta Route. Scenes along their
route from San Francisco to Portland. Dated 1934.
Mint 6.00
UP—View of Santa Barbara Mission, California. Mint 1.00
UP—Union Pacific Limited train crossing Great Salt
Lake, Utah. Mint 3.00
UP—Union Pacific streamliner, "City Of Denver."
Postmarked 1937 . . . . .2.50
WABASH—The Wabash Banner Limited—operated between
St. Louis and Chicago. Postmarked 1915 . . . . .7.50

STEREOSCOPIC VIEW CARDS

BCR&N—Passenger train wreck near Waterloo, Iowa,
dated May 28, 1899. J.P. King, Photographer 22.00
CM&StP—Passenger depot, LaCrosse, Wisconsin, 1879,
Elmer & Tenney, Winona, Minnesota,
photographer 5.00
D&RG—Passenger train the Royal Gorge near Canyon
City, Colorado, 1879. Keystone View Company,
Manufacturers-Publishers 8.00
F&PM—Express train at Clare Station, Ca. 1875,
Goodridge Bros., E. Saginaw, Michigan 15.00
M&StP—"Snowbound." No. 127—The snowed-in engine.
1873. A.L. Mckay, Decorah, Iowa 10.00
MT. WASHINGTON RY—No. 1245, Summit of Mt.
Washington, ca. 1885. Kilburn Brothers, Littleton,
New Hampshire 5.00
MT. WASHINGTON RY—No. 1825, The Great Trestle,
ca. 1885. Kilburn Brothers, Littleton, New
Hampshire 5.00
NYNH&H RR—Passenger depot, Springfield
Massachusetts ca. 1891. E. & H.T. Anthony & Co.,
New York 12.50
PRR—Engine on the Newport bridge, ca. 1870.
Purviance, Photographer, Philadelphia 25.00
PRR—Train rounding the famous Horseshoe Curve,
Allegheny mountains, Pennsylvania. ca. 1897.
Keystone View Co., Meadville, Pennsylvania 10.00
P&O—No. 2088. Passenger train at Gates of Crawford
Notch. Kilburn Brothers, Littleton, New
Hampshire 5.00

P&O—No. 2177. Passenger train on bridge, Crawford
Notch, New Hampshire. Kilburn Brothers, Littleton,
New Hampshire 5.00
W&StP—Roundhouse at Waseca, Minnesota. ca. 1881.
Elmer & Tenney, Photographers, Winona,
Minnesota 20.00

RAILROAD POSTMARKS, RPO'S

Covers bearing railroad postmarks are of interest to both the
philatelist and the railroadiana collector. Early envelopes were
postmarked with the name of the railroad on which they were
carried, and these are rare. When railway post office cars were
instituted to sort mail enroute, the envelopes bore R.P.O.
postmarks. In more recent years, anniversary, first day, and last
trip covers were issued for collectors. Many of these had special
art work and commemorative railroad postage stamps, known as
"cachet covers." There are some who make a specialty of
railroad-mail collectibles.

Special note: Many early covers bearing railroad postmarks
have high catalog value postage stamps affixed, increasing the
price of the cover considerably. Those listed here bear the more
common stamps on them with only nominal catalog value.

COVERS BEARING RAILROAD POSTMARKS

BOSTON & ALBANY RR—ca. 1853 .... 30.00
BOSTON & FITCHBURGH RR—ca. 1851 .... 40.00
MIC. CENTRAL RR—ca. 1853 .... 75.00
N.Y. & BOSTON STMB. & R.R.R—ca. 1851 .... 60.00
PROV. & STONINGTON RR—ca. 1861 .... 25.00
SOUTH. MINN. RR—ca. 1872 .... 35.00
WASHINGTON & PHILA. RR—ca. 1855 .... 50.00
W. & St. PETER R.R.—ca. 1873 .... 25.00

COVERS BEARING R.P.O. POSTMARKS

ALAMOSA & DURANGO-R.P.O. TR 216, Jan. 31, 1951,
    last trip San Juan narrow guage passenger train 3.00

Early railroad cancellation cover

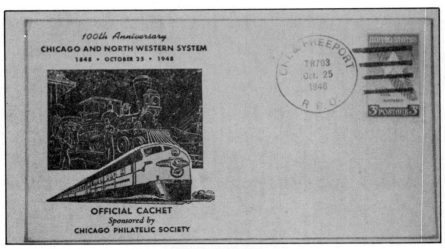

RPO cachet cover

BANGOR & BOS-R.P.O. April 11, 1898 . . . . .8.00
BROOKINGS & GETTYS-R.P.O. Dec. 30, East,
   1891 . . . . .10.00
CO. BLUFFS & K.C.-R.P.O. TR 20, Nov. 11, 1934,
   cachet, first trip Burlington Zephyr 4.50
CHI. & FREEPORT-R.P.O. TR 703, Oct. 25, 1948,
   cachet, 100th Anniversary, C&NW System 3.50

HERON LAKE & PIPESTONE-R.P.O. East, Sept. 30,
1931 . . . . .5.00
N.Y. & CHI-R.P.O. E.D. TR 51, Dec. 7, 1941, cachet,
first trip streamlined Empire State Express 4.00
PITTSBURGH & ST. LOUIS-R.P.O. TR 7, Dec. 15,
1909 . . . . .6.00
ST. ALBANS & BOSTON-R.P.O. TR 53, Mar. 1,
1894 . . . . .7.00

ROLLING STOCK RELICS

Since the demise of the Iron Horse, and when railroads stopped
running their passenger trains, there has been an increasing interest among rail buffs in preserving relics from the steam
locomotive and discontinued rolling stock. Engine bells,
headlights, whistles and such are now bringing good prices,
along with ornate brass door handle sets, fancy brass luggage
racks, ceiling and wall lamps, and so on, from passenger cars of
yesteryear. Many of these items from the vanished Iron Horse
and coaches in use during the steam era can still be found today
by the diligent collector.

BELL—steam locomotive, cast bronze, iron yoke and
stand 650.00
BRAKE WHEEL—cast iron, spoke type, 16" diameter
railroad marked, pre-1900 . . . . .65.00
CASH FARE BOX—conductors, portable, leather and
metal trim, 2½" x 5¾" x 10¼", brass hand grip,
coin slot in top, two small windows each side, "T. Ry.
Co., Pat. 1914" 175.00
DOOR HANDLE SET—coach, 2 pieces, cast brass, ornate
design, early 1900s 45.00
DRUMHEAD—rear observation car, CHICAGO
& NORTHWESTERN LINE logo at center,
NORTHWESTERN LIMITED around, 26" diameter,
electric lighted 175.00
DRUMHEAD—rear observation car, NORTHERN PACIFIC,
NORTH COAST LTD., rectangular, 28¼" x 20½",
electric lighted 300.00
FIRST AID BOX—caboose, metal, 3½" x 6" x 8½",
wall mounted, BURLINGTON ROUTE logo 30.00
HAND HOLD—coach, exterior entrance, brass bar,
length 32" 15.00

HEADLIGHT—steam locomotive, round style, electric,
   railroad marked, Pyle Natl., ca. 1920s 185.00
HERALD—diesel locomotive, metal, rectangle, 17" x 23"
   THE MILWAUKEE ROAD, white letters on red 100.00
LAMP—locomotive cab, kerosene type, complete with
   font and globe, Dietz, early 1900s 95.00
LAMP MOUNT BRACKET—caboose, marker lamps,
   cast iron, 3½" high, pair 20.00
LAMP MOUNT BRACKET—front engine classification,
   cast brass, pair, R & L side, with hole for flag mount,
   4" high 30.00
LETTER DROP CHUTE—mail car, exterior, cast iron hinged
   cover, 4" x 7" 75.00
LINK & PIN COUPLING SET—2 pieces, heavy cast
   iron, oval 4½" x 13", pin 13¾" long, UP RR,
   ca. 1880s 65.00
MAIL POUCH—Express car, canvas and leather trim,
   black stencilled letters RAILWAY EXPRESS
   AGENCY with serial number 40.00
PLAQUE—coach, stainless steel, rectangle, 5½" x 21",
   yellow and black enamel letters "S P & S" 55.00
PLAQUE—coach, brass, rectangle, 4" x 12", raised letters
   "PASSENGERS NOT ALLOWED TO STAND ON THE
   "PLATFORM" 35.00
PLAQUE—passenger car wall decor, MILWAUKEE ROAD,
   Hiawatha Indian figure cut-out, aluminum, 11½" x 19"
   oval, ½" thick 125.00
RUG—parlor car, wool, green and black floral design on
   red, large G. N. RY. goat logo in center, 27" x 46" 100.00

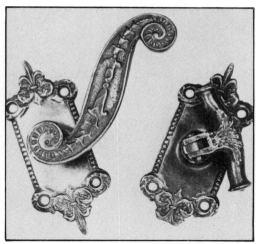

Ornate brass door handle set

Locomotive steam whistle

SEAL—Express car, metal strip 8¼" long with ball end,
  embossed "REA EXP." and serial number, unused 0.50
SEAL—box car, metal strip 8¼" long, with ball end,
  embossed with railroad initials and serial number,
  unused 1.00
SIGN—passenger car entrance, "WATCH YOUR STEP,"
  3¼" x 21", porcelainized steel, white letters on
  black 25.00
SOAP HOLDER—coach, wall type, brass, ornate, early ..18.00
SPEED RESTRICTION PLAQUE—locomotive, brass,
  1 ¾" x 5¼", cast letters, "70 MPH MAXIMUM
  PERMISSIBLE LOCOMOTIVE SPEED" 22.00
STEP BOX—passenger car, metal, embossed "GREAT
  NORTHERN" both sides, Norton Mfg. Co. Chgo 150.00
STEP BOX—Pullman, metal, embossed "PULLMAN"
  both sides, made by Utica 125.00
STEP LADDER—sleeping car, wood height 36", hinged
  back, carpeted treads, railroad marked 50.00
TICKET HOLDER—coach, wall mount type, brass, ornate
  shape, 1 3/8" x 2", incised "TICKET" and RR
  initials 15.00

STOVE—caboose, coal type, cast iron, railroad
marked 250.00
TRUST PLATE—NP, cast aluminum, 5" x 12" NORTHERN
PACIFIC RAILWAY, EQUIPMENT TRUST OF 1966,
FIRST NATIONAL CITY BANK, TRUSTEE, OWNER,
LESSOR 25.00
TRUST PLATE—C&NW, cast iron, 6½" x 16", "THE
NORTHERN TRUST COMPANY, TRUSTEE, OWNER AND
LESSOR, CHICAGO AND NORTHWESTERN RY. CO.,
THIRD EQUIP. TRUST OF 1953" 35.00

Passenger car
brass plaque

Pullman berth electric
wall lamp

WALL LAMP—Pullman berth, electric, brass, complete
with shade 45.00
WALL SHELF—coach, all brass, rectangular with rounded
front corners, grilled, 6½" x 27" 45.00

WHISTLE—caboose, back-up, all brass with lever, 8" tall,
Sherburn Co., ca. 1910 ....35.00
WHISTLE—steam locomotive, brass, triple chamber chime,
14" tall to acorn finial, Buckeye Brass Works, Dayton
Ohio 150.00
WHISTLE—steam locomotive, brass, single chamber
chime, 15" tall to finial, Powell's 125.00
WINDOW SASH LOCK—coach, brass, spring action type
with finger grips 8.00

SHEET MUSIC

Down through the years many pieces of sheet music have been
published pertaining to the railroads. "Casey Jones, The Brave
Engineer," is a classic example. Especially desirable are those
picturing the train on their colorful covers. Fine copies from the
early 1900s are in demand, steadily increasing in price. Some
sheet music was published exclusively for the railroad or
dedicated to the Brotherhoods, and these are preferred by the
more serious railroadiana collector.

Public railroad sheet music

"CASEY JONES, THE BRAVE ENGINEER"—Seibert and
Newton, 1909 ....15.00

"DOES THIS RAILROAD LEAD TO HEAVEN"—Lucy
Schleif, 1908 .... 10.00

Authentic railroad sheet music

"DREAM TRAIN"—Guy Lombardo, 1928 .... 8.50
"GUNGL'S RAILROAD GALOP," 1869, played by Willis'
band at the Mechanics' Industrial Fair 45.00
"HAIL THE BALTIMORE & OHIO"—composed and
played for the Centenary of the Railroad in 1927—
Walter Goodwin, N.Y. 12.50
"IN THE BAGGAGE COACH AHEAD"—Gussie L.
David, 1896 .... 20.00
"MAKE THAT ENGINE STOP AT LOUISVILLE"—Lewis
and Meyer, 1944 .... 5.00
"MY DAD'S THE ENGINEER"—Chas. Graham,
1895 .... 25.00
"PULLMAN PORTERS PARADE"—Maurice Abrahams
Music Co., N.Y. 1913 .... 7.50
"SONG OF THE GREAT BIG BAKED POTATO,"—
published for the Northern Pacific Ry. Dining Car Dept.,
1912 .... 22.50
"SUNSET LIMITED"—Harry J. Lincoln, Vandersloot
Music Co., 1910 .... 6.00
"THAT RAILROAD RAG"—Head Music Pub. Co., N.Y.
1911 .... 10.00

SIGNS

Ever since the railroads got out of the passenger train business, the collecting of signs that once adorned the walls of depots has proliferated. Of special interest are the various Express Company and Telegraph Company signs that hung on the outside walls of small town depots. Many were two-sided, white and blue porcelainized metal signs that could be read from both ends of the station platform. Express Company signs were also used on baggage carts. Express Company call card signs were distributed to local merchants to be displayed in the front window of their stores attracting the attention of the Express Company driver to stop and make a parcel pick-up.

Every depot had signs located at opposite ends of the building with the name of the station shown on them. The railrod serving the line also had their official logo signs posted on the outside walls of the depot. All of these miscellaneous exterior and interior signs from the vanished depots are bringing high prices today. Reproductions are being made, so be wary!

"ADAMS EXPRESS COMPANY'S MONEY ORDERS SOLD
HERE"—depot exterior, mounted flush, one-sided,
10" x 14" white on green, porcelainized steel, ca.
1900 ....250.00

Depot sign — exterior building

Depot sign — exterior door

AIR EXPRESS—"Division Railway Express Agency, Inc."
one-sided diamond shape, 8" x 8", white, black and
red, porcelainized steel, ca. 1950s 45.00

AMERICAN RAILWAY EXPRESS—call card, diamond
shape, two-sided, 14" x 14", red, white and green,
heavy cardboard with metal rims, grommeted hole at top,
ca. 1920s 100.00

BURLINGTON ROUTE—depot exterior logo, mounted
flush, rectangular, 21" x 27", white, black and red,
heavy steel, stamped "CB&Q RR" on back side 150.00

"DEER CREEK"—depot exterior station name sign,
mounted flush, 12" x 66" long, black on white, heavy
steel 50.00

GREAT NORTHERN—"WAITING ROOM," depot
interior, 10" x 26", wood, white letters on black 35.00

NORTHERN PACIFIC—"NOTICE! The Value Of All
Baggage Must Be Declared In Writing." depot interior,
10" x 13", cardboard, 1948 . . . . .15.00

NORTHERN PACIFIC—"PARCEL CHECK ROOM Inquire
At Ticket Window," depot interior, 7" x 11", cardboard,
1946 . . . . .15.00

Depot sign — inside wall

"PUBLIC TELEPHONE"—depot exterior, hanging, two-sided, 18" x 18", bell in center, blue on white, porcelainized steel 35.00

RAILWAY EXPRESS AGENCY—"PACKAGES RECEIVED HERE"—depot exterior, hanging, two-sided, 15" x 18", red diamond on white, black letters at bottom, porcelainized steel 75.00

RAILWAY EXPRESS AGENCY—depot exterior, mounted flush, one-sided, 11½" x 72" long, yellow letters on black, porcelainized steel 125.00

RAILWAY EXPRESS AGENCY—baggage cart, one-sided, diamond shape, 14" x 14", white, black and red, porcelainized steel, 1950s 30.00

UNION PACIFIC SYSTEM—TICKETS FOR CHILDREN— "Under the law, children 5 years old and under 12 must pay Half Fare; 12 years or over, Full Fare." depot interior, 8" x 10", white and blue porcelainized steel, 1930s 100.00

WELLS FARGO & CO. EXPRESS—call card, diamond shape, two-sided, 14" x 14", black, white and red, heavy cardboard with metal rims, grommeted hole at top, ca. 1920s 250.00

"WESTERN UNION TELEGRAPH AND CABLE OFFICE"— depot exterior, hanging, two-sided, 12" x 24", white on blue, porcelainized steel 85.00

"WESTERN UNION TELEGRAPH AND CABLE OFFICE"— depot exterior door, mounted flush, one-sided, 4" x 9", white on blue, porcelainized steel, 1930s 35.00

WESTERN UNION TELEGRAPH AND CABLE OFFICE"— depot exterior, hanging, two-sided, 11" x 16", globe center, white on dark blue, porcelainized steel 65.00

"WESTERN UNION TELEGRAMS"—depot exterior, hanging, two-sided, 10" x 17", white on dark blue, porcelainized steel 55.00

SMOKING ACCESSORIES

Millions of book matches were handed out freely by the railroads, having their logos, named trains, and colorful advertising printed on their covers. Those from the steam era are especially desired and are worth more. Countless numbers of ashtrays were used on the diners, smoking, and parlor cars, and in the railroad's ticket offices and depots. These were made of glass, ceramic, and metal, in various shapes and sizes, with the railroad's logo prominently displayed. The older ashtrays are more in demand and priced higher.

The small, pocket-type cigarette lighters with the railroad's name or logo on them are collectible and moderately priced. Those from several decades past sell for more. The railroad marked spittoons or cuspidors from the early days are also sought after by collectors. The all-brass cuspidor is the most popular and brings a high price.

Book matches

ASHTRAYS

ACL—Glass, 3¼" square, white/blue logo 7.50
B&O—Glass, 4½" square, capitol dome logo 7.00
C&O—China, Buffalo, rectangular 3½" x 7½", Geo.
    Washington silhouette 85.00
ERIE—Glass, 4½" square, white/blue logo 7.00
GN—China, Syracuse, round 4" diameter, mountain,
    goat, evergreens on white 65.00
GN—Porcelain, P&S, round 4½" diameter, black, gold
    goat logo center 35.00
L&N—Glass, hexagon, 5", red logo 8.00
M&StL—Glass, 3½" square, red/black logo 15.00
M&StL—Ceramic, round, 5½" diameter, white logo and
    letters on blue 45.00
NP—Glass, 4¾" square, Yellowstone Park Line logo 13.50

146

Cigarette case and lighter

NP—Glass, 4¾" square, monad logo 10.00
NP—Glass, octagon 5" x 5", monad logo 12.00
PRR—Glass, 3½" square, red Keystone logo 6.00
ROCK ISLAND—Glass, 4¼" square, red logo 7.50
SAL—Glass, 3½" square, heart logo 8.00
SOO LINE—Blue glass, round 4½" diameter, 3 logos around
    edge 15.00
SOO LINE—Glass, 4" square, white/red logo 7.50
SOO LINE—Metal, black finish, round 6" diameter, red
    logo in raised center 15.00
SR—Glass, 3½" square, green logo 10.00
T&P—China, Hall, oval 4" x 6", gold logo on cobalt
    blue, matchbox holder center 55.00
UP—Blue glass, round 4½" dia., Sun Valley, Idaho,
    Utah Parks 9.50
C&NW—Floorstand model, 26" high, cast iron, chrome/
    black finish, logo on base 150.00

BOOK MATCHES — (Complete with matches unless otherwise noted)

ACL—Logo, list of name trains, silver printing on
    purple 0.75
AA—Flag logo, "Double A Service," red and blue
    printing on white 0.50
B&O—Gold logo on blue, list of name trains backside
    (cover only) 1.25
BURLINGTON ROUTE—Zephyr, list of name trains, silver
    background 1.50
CPR—Beaver atop red shield logo, gold background 1.25
CMStP&P—Red logo, Hiawatha streamliner #1 ....1.25
C&NW—Logo and streamliner, "400" fleet 1.00
ERIE—Logo and diesel streamliner, yellow printing on blue
    (cover only) 0.75

FRISCO LINES—Black logo on yellow, against red
stripes 0.50
GN—Logo and Indian, "Route Of The Empire
Builder" 1.25
GB&W—Red logo and diesel on black with yellow lines
(cover only) 0.75
IC—Diamond logo and black steam locomotive on green
and gold 2.50
LACKAWANNA—Gold logo, "Route of Phoebe Snow," on
maroon 0.50
MO-PAC—Hounddog, route of the Eagles logo, yellow
background 1.75
NICKEL PLATE ROAD—Logo, "NKP" on map, blue printing
on cream 0.75
NYC—The James Whitcomb Riley diesel streamliner, blue
logo (cover only) 2.00
NYO&W—W logo, white printing on dark blue (cover
only) 0.75
NP—Yellowstone Park Line logo on red background 2.00
N&W—Streamline steam train, Pocahontas and
Cavalier 2.00
PRR—1846-1946, 100 year emblem, gold on maroon 1.75
QUANAH ROUTE—Logo, Indian chief, purple and
white (cover only) 1.50
RIO GRANDE—Logo and advertising, black printing on red
(cover only) 1.00
ROCK ISLAND—Black logo on red 0.35
SANTA FE—Chico Indian boy holding logo, black on
white 0.35

**Minneapolis &
St. Louis ceramic
ashtray**

SP—Stylized daylight streamliner on yellow 1.50
T&P—Red logo on green background (cover only) 1.35
UP—Gold shield log on red 0.25
WABASH—Red flag logo on dark blue (cover only) 1.25

CIGARETTE LIGHTERS

A&S—Locomotive, logo, Agent's name, black/red
   on silver, Rolex 15.00
FRISCO—Logo, map of system, gold on red, Vulcan 12.50
GN—Logo, diesel train, red/black on silver, "GN" 10.00
SOO LINE—Logo both sides, white on maroon,
   Warren 8.50
SANTA FE—Chico Indian boy, logo, red on gold,
   WindMaster 5.00

CUSPIDORS

MO-PAC—Metal, white enamel with black "MO-PAC"
   on side rim, 7¼" top diameter, 5" tall 47.00
PULLMAN—Nickel finish on brass, "PULLMAN COMPANY"
   on bottom, 7" diameter, 3" tall 45.00
SOO LINE—Brass, raised logo on cast iron bottom,
   9" top diameter, 7½" tall 125.00
UP—White porcelainized steel, black "UNION PACIFIC"
   on inside rim, 8" top diameter, 5" tall 47.00

STATIONERY ITEMS

There are numerous items that the collector can search for in this
category. Pencils and pens carrying railroad logos, blotters
featuring vacation spots and "name" passenger trains, rulers
with interesting advertising slogans, scratch pads, letterheads
and envelopes, etc., all were once produced in large quantities
and widely distributed. Railroad-marked stationery items are
now getting scarce and prices on them are on the rise.

BALL POINT PENS

BN—green logo on white, "Tucker, USA" 1.00
DM&IR—maroon initials on gold, "Readyriter" 3.00
MO-PAC—red logo, black train on pearlized,"Quick Point,
   St. Louis" 6.00
NP—black logo on blue, "Rite-O-Graph, USA" 1.50
SOO LINE—gold logo on black, "Wings, USA" 2.00

PEN POINTS

CGW RY—steel pen point with wood holder, cork grip 3.00
GN RY—steel pen point with wood holder 2.00

M&StL RR—steel pen point with wood holder, cork
grip 3.00
NYNH&H RR—steel pen point, without holder 1.00
N&W RY—steel pen point, without holder 1.00

PENCILS — wood, with graphite "leads" — unused

BCR&N RY—gold printing on maroon, round, no eraser
(rare) 12.50
BN—white printing on green, hexagon, eraser 0.35
C&O—black printing on chrome yellow, round 0.35
CGW—gold printing on green, hexagon, eraser 3.50
C&NW—gold printing on maroon, round, no eraser 1.00
CStPM&O—gold printing on black, round, no
eraser 2.50
KCS—silver printing on tan, round, no eraser 1.25
MILWAUKEE ROAD—silver printing on green, round,
no eraser 1.00
MO-PAC—white printing on maroon, hexagon,
eraser 0.35
MC&StL—green printing on yellow, hexagon, eraser 0.35
N&W—silver printing on tan, round, no eraser 0.35
ROCK ISLAND LINES—white letters on red, round, no
eraser 0.35
SANTA FE—gold letters on maroon, round, no eraser 0.35
SOO LINE—gold letters on tan, round, no eraser 2.00
WABASH—flag logo, blue letters on white, round
fat pencil, eraser 5.00

PENCILS, MECHANICAL

C&NW—green printing on yellow, green ends,
"Redipoint" 7.50
FRISCO—gold logo and printing on black, gold
ends, "Ritepoint" 5.00
GN—logo on pearlized, black ends, no manufacturer 10.00
MILWAUKEE ROAD—Hiawatha steam train, red logo on
pearlized, "Quickpoint, St. Louis" 12.50
M&STL—diesel freight on white, black ends,
"Redipoint" 15.00
PULLMAN-STANDARD CAR MFG. CO.—white
printing on maroon, black ends, "Autopoint" 8.00
RIO GRANDE—logo, red and black, pearlized, no
manufacturer 10.00
ROCK ISLAND—Rocket streamliner, red logos, pearlized,
no manufacturer 10.00

SAL RY—black printing on white, black ends, "Scripto" 5.00
SOO LINE—red logo, pearlized, "Quickpoint, St. Louis" 12.00

Inkwells

RULERS

C&NW—15" wood, logos front, diesel trains back, 1940s 10.00
CGW—12" plastic, logo at center, black printing on white 8.00
GM&O—12" plastic, logos, diesel freight, map, red & black printing on white 3.00
GN—8" celluloid on tin, logo, 1931 calendar, black printing on white 12.00
KCS—15" wood, "Port Arthur Route" front, "Straight As The Crow Flies" map backside 1903 (rare) 35.00
SOO LINE—12" enameled tin, logo, map, red printing on white 5.00

BLOTTERS

C&NW—"The Train For Comfort—The Northwestern Ltd." ca. 1905 ....5.00
CStP&KC—Iron horse with wings galloping down track, ca. 1889 ....12.50
CStPM&O—Fireman shoveling coal in engine cab, ca. 1895 ....10.00
GN—Chief Two Guns White Calf, 1932 ....2.50

NYC—20th Century Ltd." and railroad stations,
1930s 3.50
N&W—Wharf scenes, three calendar months, 1938 ....2.00
NP—"Famous For Food—The Great Big Baked Potato,"
ca. 1930s 3.00
SP—Map of system, three calendar months, 1926 ....4.00
UP—Grand, Zion, Bryce Canyon National Parks,
1930s 2.75
WABASH—Lady seated in coach, logo, orange and
blue, 1920s 5.00

STATIONERY — Tourist

BURLINGTON—sheet of paper & envelope "Denver
Zephyr" 1.00
GN—sheet of paper, 8½" x 11" 0.25
GN—sheet of paper and envelope, "The Oriental
Limited" 3.00
C&NW—sheet of paper, 8½" x 11" 0.25
IC—envelope, regular size, 3½" x 6" 0.25
LV—envelope, business size, 4" x 9½" 0.35

Miscellaneous stationery items

MILWAUKEE ROAD—sheet of paper & envelope, "Route
Of The Hiawathas" 2.00
ROCK ISLAND—sheet of paper & envelope, "Route Of
The Rockets" 2.00
SANTA FE—sheet of paper & envelope, "The Chief
Way" 1.00

MISCELLANEOUS

D&RGW—scratch pad, picture of diesel freight in
Rocky Mountains 1.50
M&STL—scratch pad, logo and modern diesel freight
locomotive 3.00
P RR—glass inkwell, metal cover, both marked
"P RR" 22.50
P RR—glass postage stamp moistener, sponge insert,
bottom marked "P RR" 18.00
SANTA FE—scratch pad, logo and blue line drawings
of diesels on white 1.00
SOO LINE—metal scratch pad holder, 4" x 8½", clip at
top with logo 8.00

STOCKS, BONDS AND CURRENCY

Railroad stock and bond certificates date back to the early days
of the railroads, usually having the locomotive in their designs.
Some of the engraving companies that did this work went out of
business long ago. Many of these certificates feature a magnifi-
cent engine vignette and beautiful ornate scrollwork. There are
collectors who specialize only in these. Some railroads issued

Stock certificate

their own currency, which was also a work of art. These interesting paper collectibles of years ago are in demand today.

STOCKS

B&O—100 shares Common, Tom Thumb train vignette,
brown border, issued 1903, cancelled 4.50
BO&SW—10 shares Preferred, train and depot in small
circle, green border, issued 1894, cancelled 4.75
CW&B—10 shares Common, allegorical children, locomotive
in center oval, 1880s, unissued 10.00

**Early
mortgage bond**

CB&Q—100 shares Capital, locomotive vignette, brown
border, issued 1895, cancelled 3.50
CGW—100 shares Preferred, allegorical figures, train
in center circle, rust border, issued 1965,
cancelled 4.75

154

C&NW—100 shares Common, winged mythological figures
each side of railroad's herald in center, issued 1958,
cancelled 3.75
CStPM&O—20 shares Common, locomotive in center, brown
border, issued 1922, cancelled 5.00
GM&N—100 shares Common, trains in center oval, brown
border, issued 1929, cancelled 5.00
GM&O—100 shares Common, allegorical figures, train in
center frame, blue border, issued 1941, cancelled 4.75
H&NH—5 shares Capital, woodcut locomotive and ship,
black border. issued 1846, cancelled. (rare) 20.00
M&StL—100 shares Captial, allegorical female and
locomotive vignette, purple border, early 1900s,
unissued 2.50
MK&T—10 shares Capital, cattle vignette, violet border,
issued 1887, cancelled 7.50
MK&T—100 shares Common, locomotive and roundhouse
vignette, green border, issued 1907, cancelled 4.50

BONDS

HARTFORD, PROVIDENCE & FISHKILL RR CO.—
$1,000 bond, primitive train one end, embossed
seal, issued 1854, redeemed 15.00

Early railroad currency

SOUTH MOUNTAIN RAILROAD CO.—$500.00 gold bond, train on bridge vignette, dated 1873, unissued, all coupons intact 12.50

TROY & GREENFIELD RR CO.—$1,000 bond, early train, dated 1854, unissued, all coupons intact 17.50

UTAH & PLEASANT VALLEY RAILWAY CO.—$1,000 gold bond, miners, industry and train in center oval, issued 1878, partially redeemed 12.00

CURRENCY

BRUNSWICK & ALBANY RR CO—$2.00, bank building obverse, train and depot vignette reverse, 1871 .... 12.00

CENTRAL RAILROAD & BANKING CO. OF GEORGIA— $2.00, cut of early train, 1861 .... 5.00

ERIE & KALAMAZOO RAILROAD BANK—$1.00, ships vignette in center, 1853 .... 15.00

ERIE & KALAMAZOO RAILROAD BANK—$10.00, vignette of people waving to passing train, 1854 .... 15.00

MISSISSIPPI & ALABAMA RR CO—Figures and train in center vignette, portraits each corner, 1837 .... 30.00

MISSISSIPPI CENTRAL RR CO—25¢, early passenger train, 1862 .... 4.00

MISSISSIPPI & TENNESSEE RR CO—5¢, vignette Indians left side, American eagle center, 1862 .... 4.00

SOUTH CAROLINA RAILROAD CO—$2.00, early locomotive vignette in center, 1800s, uncirculated 3.00

VIRGINIA CENTRAL RAILROAD CO—$10.00, funnel stack train vignette, 1861 .... 6.00

WESTERN & ATLANTIC RR—50¢, early train printed in red, 1862 .... 3.50

TELEPHONES, TELEGRAPHY, INSULATORS

The most popular item with the collector of this category is the key and sounder. Those railroad-marked are especially preferred. The telephone was also a part of the station agent's equipment, which included the scissors phone, candlestick desk phone, box-type wall phone, bell boxes, and miscellaneous related accessories. A lineman's portable phone with its case and shoulder strap is also included. All of this old depot telegraph and telephone equipment is collectible today. Prices vary depending on condition.

Glass insulators used on telegraph poles are also a part of this category, and the collecting of them has grown rapidly in the last decade. They were made in various colors, the most common being shades of green and blue. These are generally marked with the manufacturer's name, and many have patent dates. Those

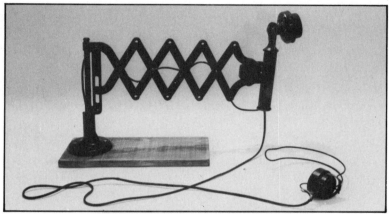

Scissors phone — desk mount style

Dispatcher's wall phone and bell box

that are railroad-marked are of special interest to the railroadiana collector. Value depends on condition and rarity.

TELEPHONES

DESK PHONE—candlestick type, 12" tall, handset earpiece receiver, "American Tel. & Tel. Co. Pat. Jan. 14, 1913" 110.00

DESK PHONE—dial in oval base, 5" tall, handset mouthpiece and ear receiver, "Western Elec. Co., ca. 1930-1940" 55.00

PORTABLE PHONE—lineman's, leather case with shoulder strap 95.00

SCISSORS PHONE—desk mount style, with hook and headset receiver, "Western Electric, Pat. 1915" 155.00

WALL PHONE—oak box 6½" x 9", with "Push to Talk, Release to Listen" button, hook and headset receiver, "W.E. Co." 65.00

WALL PHONE—long box type, oak, 9½" x 20½", hook and headset receiver, "Push to Talk" button. "Western Electric" 185.00

BELL BOX—oak, 6½" x 9", railroad marked, two bells on top, "Western Electric, type 295A" 45.00

DISPATCHERS TRANSMITTER HORN—with neck strap and cord, "Western Electric" 37.50

JACK-HOLE BOX—oak, 4½" x 6¼", three plugs, "W.E. Co." 25.00

PEG BOARD—wood panel 18" x 22", ten position type with twenty pegs or plugs, marked "Western Elec. Co." 200.00

PEG BOARD—wood panel 13" x 9½", four position type with nine pegs, "Marked Bunnell W.U. Tel. Co." 135.00

TELEGRAPHY

KEY—Yellow brass base, oval, railroad marked, "Chas. Cory & Sons, N.Y." 40.00

KEY—Yellow brass base, oval, not RR marked, "J.H. Bunnell & Co., N.Y." 65.00

KEY—Vibroplex, cast iron base, rectangular, brass maker's plate with serial number, side-swiper style key for high speed sending 75.00

RELAY—Cast iron base, rectangular, railroad marked, 150 OHMS, "J.H. Bunnell & Co., N.Y." 55.00

RESONATOR—Two adjustable cast iron arms, triangle shaped wood box, "White Co., Worcester, Mass., Pat. Aug. 7, 1911" 130.00

Sounder mounted in swivel arm resonator

Telegraph key

RESONATOR—Three adjustable cast iron arms, triangle
shaped wood box, "White Co., Worcester, Mass.,
Pat. Aug. 7, 1911" 150.00
RESONATOR—Stationary, curved back wood box mounted
on iron pole 9" tall, no maker's name 25.00
RESONATOR—Stationary model as above, complete with
sounder 65.00

SOUNDER—Yellow brass, rectangle, mounted on wood
base, railroad marked, "J.H. Bunnell & Co. N.Y.,
Pat. May 7, 1895" 45.00
SOUNDER—Yellow brass, rectangle, mounted on wood
base, not railroad marked, "J.H. Bunnell & Co.
N.Y.," no pat. date 35.00
BOOK—*Manual of Railway Commercial And Wireless
Telegraphy,* by Fred L. Meyer, Seventh Edition,
1914 .... 30.00
BOOK—*Telegraphy Code, Mobile & Ohio RR.,* issued
St. Louis, May 10, 1920, soft cover 25.00
SIGN—Counter style, easel back, 5½" x 9", "Western
Union Telegrams" on dark blue, porcelainized
metal 35.00

Glass insulators

INSULATORS

B&O—aqua glass, "B&O" and "pat. Jan. 25, 1870"
raised on dome 25.00
B&O—white porcelain, "B&O" indented on base 13.00
CNR—white porcelain, "CNR" raised on dome 15.00
CPR—light blue glass, raised letters around base 15.00
CPR—light green glass, raised letters around base 15.00
CPR—amethyst glass, raised letters around base 17.50
PRR—aqua green glass, raised initials on top of
dome 10.00
PRR—dark green glass, raised initials on top of
dome 12.00

TICKETS AND RELATED ITEMS

The railroads used a great variety of tickets down through the years. The colorful printed tickets in use before the turn of the century by roads long gone are in greater demand and bring high prices. Many collectors specialize in the small, card-stock tickets, from as many different railroads as possible. Also included are the small envelopes given travelers to protect their tickets. The earlier steam era envelopes were later replaced by folder types having an inside pocket, with the advent of the diesel. Those featuring named trains are especially desirable. Every conductor had his own ticket punch, which had particular markings in the die to perforate the tickets. The collector can accumulate any number of these old ticket punches, each with a different die mark. Ticket punches that are railroad marked are priced higher.

Cardstock tickets

Validators were used in the railroad's ticket offices to stamp the railroad's name, location, and date on the traveler's ticket, validating it. Those from the last century in good condition, complete with ribbon and die, have greater value. Spare dies for these machines can also be found, and they are priced according to the rarity of the railroad's name on them. Rubber hand stamps used in depots to imprint additional words in ink on the ticket, such as "First Class," "One Way Coach," named train,

161

town, etc., are now being picked up too. Another item to look for in this category is the small cardboard seat check the conductor gave the passenger when he picked up the ticket. Those from

Miscellaneous
tickets

before the turn of the century are scarce and hard to come by. Last but not least: Don't overlook the ticket cabinets with roll-down fronts used in small town depots years ago.

TICKETS

B&M—Commutation, five rides, card type, 1892 . . . . 3.00
BURLINGTON ROUTE—Commutation, ten rides, local, card
   type, 1900 . . . . 2.50
CV—Mileage ticket, 500 miles, folded type, cardboard,
   1886 . . . . 4.00
C&NW—Emigrant passage, coupon strip with stub, paper,
   1877 . . . . 7.50
C&NW—1000 mile coupon booklet, partially used,
   1886 . . . . 6.00
CGW—1000 mile ticket booklet, unused, 1903 . . . . 5.00
CM&StP—Cash fare receipt, paper, 1927 . . . . 2.00
CNS&M—Child's half-fare ticket, local, cardstock,
   unissued 0.50
CStP&KC—Half-fare ticket, local, paper stock,
   1893 . . . . 4.00

ERR—Commutation, 60 rides, Allendale and New York,
card type, 1921 ....1.50
FITCHBURG RR—One First Class passage, local, with stub,
cardboard, 1880 ....4.00
GN—One First Class passage, local, card stock, 1922 .....1.25
GN—First Class half-fare permit, St. Paul to Duluth,
paper, 1900 ....2.50
MP—Excursion ticket, Leavenworth-Kansas City, paper,
1902 ....1.50
MP—Carbonized ticket booklet, paper stock, unused,
1960 ....2.00
MONON—Carbonized ticket booklet, paper stock, unused,
1960s 2.00
NYC&StL—One First Class passage, local, card stock,
1886 ....3.00
NYLE&W—One First Class passage, local, card stock,
1893 ....1.75
NYNH&H—One passage half-fare, local, card stock,
1890 ....2.25
NP—One First Class passage, local, card stock, 1891 ......2.00
NP—25 ride individual commutation ticket book, local,
unissued, 1920s 5.00
PRR—Coach ticket, local, card stock, 1926 ....1.50
ROCK ISLAND—One way coach reservation ticket on the
Rocket, card stock, 1942 ....1.50

Diesel era ticket envelopes

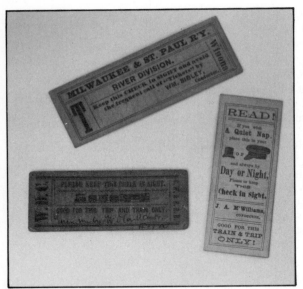

Early cardstock seat checks

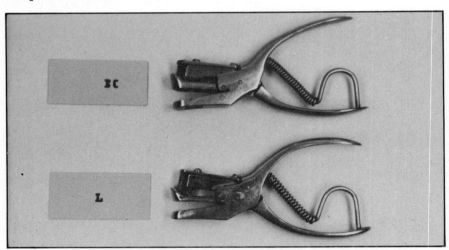

Conductor's ticket punches

SOO LINE—Six month round trip coach ticket with stub, paper stock, 1951 .... 1.50
SOO LINE—Banana messenger's ticket book, coupons for 10 trips, partially used, 1930s. Scarce 10.00
W&StP—First Class, local, card stock, unused, 1879 ...... 6.00

TICKET ENVELOPES

B&O—Train at depot frontside, system map/logo back,
blue-white envelope, 1940s 2.00
C&O—Chessie kitten frontside, map/logo back, green-
white envelope, 1940s 2.00
GN—Logo/Empire Builder front and back, blue-white
folder, 1960s 1.00
IC—5 named diesel trains frontside, system map/logo
back, white-rust envelope, 1950s 1.50
MILWAUKEE ROAD—Views of Superdome Hiawathas and
logos both sides, yellow envelope, 1960s 1.00
MO-PAC—Eagle diesel streamliner frontside, logo/flying
Eagle back, red-black envelope, 1950s 2.00
NYC—Old State House, Boston, frontside, logos back,
green-white envelope, 1950s 1.50
NP—Dome cars under semaphore signals frontside, logo
back, red folder, 1960s 1.00
ROCK ISLAND—Logo/Rocket frontside, logo/map
backside, red envelope, 1960s 1.25

Miscellaneous rubber stamps

TICKET PUNCHES

B&M—Fleur-de-lis punch mark, "pat. July 18,
1882" 20.00
CGW—"L" punch mark 12.50

CNW—"½" punch mark 12.50
GN—"2d" punch mark 14.00
NYC—"B" punch mark 12.50
PRR—"L" punch mark, "Pat. Dec. 23, 1884" 18.00
Unmarked—heart punch mark 6.00
Unmarked—clover punch mark 6.00
Unmarked—crescent punch mark .6.00
Unmarked—star punch mark 6.00
Unmarked—dual marking, star and shoe 8.50
Unmarked—satellite punch mark and edge cutter
   pattern 8.50

Ticket validater

TICKET DATER VALIDATING MACHINES

HILL'S MODEL A—Centennial dater, complete with die and
   ribbon. "Great Northern Railway, Anoka, Minn."
   Dates 1946-1957 . . . . .85.00
HILL'S MODEL A-D—Centennial dater, complete with die
   and ribbon. "Nor. Pac. Ry.   Little Falls, Minn."
   Dates 1952-1963 . . . . .75.00
COSMO MODEL NO. 2—Complete with die and ribbon.
   "C.R.I. & P Ry. Lewis, Ia." Dates 1910-1959 . . . . .55.00
COSMO MODEL NO. 3—Complete with die and ribbon.
   "Erie R.R. Co. Decatur, Ind." Dates 1910-1969 . . . . .65.00

SPARE TICKET DATER DIES

"CMSt P&P RR, Glenview, Ill." 40.00
"CM&StP RY, SOO LINE, CRI&P RY, Mpls. Depot"
   (triple marked) 65.00

"CRI&P RY, Hope, Minn." 35.00
"GN RY, Pekin, N.D." 40.00
"IC RR. 9279, Albany, La." 30.00
"MO PAC RR CO—Prescott, Ark." 37.50
"NO.PAC.RY—Ritzville, Wash." 45.00

TICKET CABINETS

Oak, slanted roll front, large size 36" high, Pool Bros.
  Mfgrs. 275.00
Oak, verticle roll front, small size, 8" x 15" x 28",
  National Ticket Case Co. 200.00

RUBBER HAND STAMPS

"ONE WAY COACH"—Black upright handle atop
  rectangular rubber die base 2.50
"ONE WAY FIRST CLASS"—Black upright handle atop
  rectangular rubber die base 2.50
"ROOMETTE"—One piece finger-molded narrow rubber
  die 1.00
"EMPIRE BUILDER"—Name train, one piece finger-molded
  narrow rubber die 1.00
"LACROSSE"—Town name, one piece finger-molded
  narrow rubber die 0.75

SEAT CHECKS

BCR&M—1870s, blue cardstock 4.00
C&NW, Dakota Division—1870s, lavendar cardstock 2.25
M&StP, River Division—1870s, yellow cardstock 3.00
NY&E—1870s, orange cardstock, cut of train 3.50
NYNH&H—1870s, green cardstock, cut of train 3.50
W&StP—1870s, green cardstock 4.00

Spare dies

TIMETABLES

Many collectors price timetables on a yearly scale, starting with a base price for the most recent date and increasing each previous year to 1900 by a nominal amount, making exceptions for the uncommon. The colorful timetables previous to the 1940s, picturing trains, legendary figures, ornate logos, and interesting slogans on their covers, generally bring the higher prices, as do those from short lines, narrow gauge, and defunct roads. The pictorial timetables of the last half of the nineteenth century are highly prized and have greater value. Many of these were a large single sheet with a colored map on one side, with illustrations, advertising and train schedules on the other side, folding into a pamphlet. The earliest timetables, such as the small card or single sheet of paper listing train schedules, are the rarities.

Employee timetables also evolved from a single sheet to booklet and folder types. They were issued for employees only, containing restricted information as to the operation of the trains, and were never distributed to the general public. Those from early, now defunct roads have a higher value. Some collectors specialize in employee timetables only.

New York and New Haven Railroad Time Table, 1855.

Early card-type timetables

168

ALTON RAILROAD—1932, May 29, engineer and fireman in
cab 8.00
AMTRAK—1972, Jan. 16 ....1.00
AT&SF—1882, Dec. 21, pictorial fold-out 30.00
ACL—1951, Sept. 30 ....3.00
B&O—1884, June 15, pictorial fold-out 32.00
B&O—1936, April 26 ....5.00
B&OSW—1911, No. 1 ....8.50
BIG FOUR ROUTE—1936, June 1, Cincinnati Union
Terminal 5.00
B&A—1903, Jan. 12, South Station, local 9.50
B&M—1879, June 30, Summer Arrangement, folder 15.00
B&M—1910, June 20, local 7.50
B&M—1928, Oct. 29, Minute Man 5.00
BN—1970, Oct. 25 ....1.00
BURLINGTON ROUTE—1930, July-August 6.00
CPR. 1913, Feb. 1, beaver and shield 12.50
CV—1913, July 1 ....10.00
C&O—1909, May 23 ....10.00
C&A—1882, Feb., pictorial fold-out 30.00
CB&Q—1878, Feb-June, pictorial fold-out 35.00
C&EI—1948, Dec. 12, Georgia streamliner 3.00
CM&StP—1897, Aug. 1, dining car interior 15.00
CMStP&P—1937, June-July 5.00
C&NW—1882, Nov. 12, pictorial fold-out 30.00
C&NW—1900, Dec. 9, passenger train 13.50
C&NW—1939, April 30, "400" and streamliners 4.00
CStP&KC—1889, July 28, maple leaf emblem (scarce) 25.00
CGW—1912, Mar. 1, Corn Belt emblem 10.00
COLORADO MIDLAND—1909, July 22.50
D&H—1907, Summer, train at night 10.00
D&RG—1893, Sept., pictorial fold-out 15.00
D&RGW—1951, June 1, Royal Gorge 4.00
DM&N—1912, July, No. 39 ....12.50
DSS&A—1940, Dec. 15 ....6.00
ERIE—1906, June 24 ....10.00
FITCHBURG RAILROAD—1884, Dec., pictorial fold-out
(rare) 35.00
FEC—1951, Sept. 30, diesel 3.00
FRISCO SYSTEM—1903, February 10.00
GTP—1915, June 6 ....8.50
GN—1901, July 15, Cascade tunnel 12.00
GN—1916, May 14, local 7.50
GN—1930, June, mountain goat logo 5.00
GN—1948, Oct-Nov-Dec., streamliners 3.00
GM&O—1947, December 3.00

Folding single sheet timetables—pre-1900

HARLEM EXTENSION RR—1871, May 29, single sheet,
  woodcut of primitive train. (rare) 65.00
IC—1899, April 20, Southern Fast Mail emblem 15.00
IR—1938, Sept. 6, electric train 6.00
IRON MOUNTAIN ROUTE—1885, Oct. 20, pictorial
  fold-out 25.00
JCRR—1944, March 12 .... 3.50
KCS—1947, June 22, "Southern Belle" streamliner 3.00
LACKAWANNA RAILROAD—1901, Sept. 1 .... 11.50
LACKAWANNA RAILROAD—1952, Sept. 28, "Phoebe
  Snow" streamliner 3.00
LS&MS—1857, Mar. 31, card type (rare) 50.00
LS&MS—1878, May 12, pictorial fold-out 35.00
LS&MS—1901, Jan., Fast Mail sack 12.50
LV—1905, May 14 .... 10.00
L&N—1944, Dec. 17 .... 3.50
MEC—1899, May 1, pictorial fold-out 15.00
MEX. NAT. RR—1897, Sept. 9 .... 16.00
M&StL—1907, June 2, "Albert Lea Route" logo 12.50
MKT—1901, Jan., figure of "Katy" 15.00
MP—1946, Nov. 24, "Eagles" streamliner 3.50
M&O—1914, Nov. 22 .... 8.00
MONON ROUTE—1946, Nov. 17 .... 3.00
NC&StL—1947, Spring 2.00
NAT.RYS.MEX—1929, Oct-Nov 7.50
NEW HAVEN RAILROAD—1967, April 30 .... 1.00
NY&NH RR—1855, card type (rare) 50.00
NYC—1931, Sept. 27, passenger train 5.00
NYC&HR—1884, Nov. 11, pictorial fold-out 30.00

NICKEL PLATE—1893, May 28, pictorial fold-out 15.00
N&W—1953, June 7 . . . . .3.00
NP—1880, Sept. (rare) 45.00
NP—1887, July, pictorial fold-out .27.50
NP—1929, Feb-Mar 6.00
PC—1971, March 3 . . . . .0.75
PRR—1887, March 23, pictorial fold-out 25.00
PRR—1945, Sept. 30, turntable 3.50
PRR—1963, Feb. 10 . . . . .1.50
PM—1946, Aug. 10, "Pere Marquette" streamliner 3.00
P&R—1903, Nov. 29, P & R emblem, fold-out 12.00
READING RAILWAY SYSTEM—1947, Sept. 28 . . . . .3.00
ROCK ISLAND—1924, June 22 . . . . .6.00
RUT—1913, June 22 . . . . .13.00
SL&SW—1947, Dec. 21 . . . . .3.00
StP&D—1899, Spring, pictorial fold-out (rare) 25.00
StPM&M—1886, July, pictorial fold-out (rare) 35.00
SEABOARD RAILWAY—1945, Jan. 15 . . . . .3.00
SOO LINE—1905, Aug. 1, local 12.50
SOO LINE—1915, March 17 . . . . .12.00
SOO LINE—1963, Dec. 10 . . . . .1.50
SP—1912, Dec., Sunset Ogden & Shasta Route logo 10.00
SP—1970, Oct. 20 . . . . .0.75
SR—1951, Aug. 5, "Crescent" & "Southerner"
streamliners 3.00

Steam era timetables

SP&S—1957, Jan. 1 . . . . .4.00
STONINGTON LINE BOAT AND RAIL—1880, Summer,
pictorial fold-out (rare) 37.50

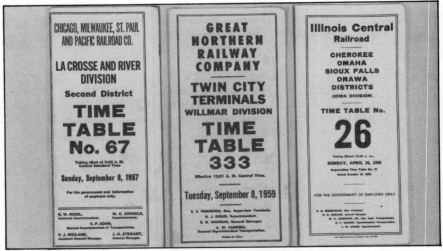

Employee timetables

EMPLOYEE TIMETABLES

TOOLS, STEAM ERA VINTAGE

Collecting old railroad-marked tools from the steam era, used by workers in the roundhouses, shops, depots and for track maintenance, has become a hobby for many. Some specialize in the small hand-tools only, while others collect all types, both large and small. The railroad marking is found somewhere on the metal or the wood handle.

"AT&SF RY"—Cold steel chisel, 8" long 7.00
"B&M RR"—Ax, "TRUE TEMPER," 30" handle 35.00
"C&NW"—Monkey wrench, all metal, size 18, "TRIMO,"
 16" long 12.50
"C&NW"—Double headed open ended curved wrench,
 10" long 9.00
"CB&Q"—Track shovel, "HUSKEY" 15.00
"CB&Q"—Steel rail splitter, V shape, "ONA," head
 8" long 8.00

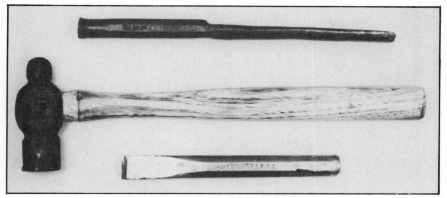

Ball pein hammer and chisels

"CM&StP RY"—Monkey wrench, all metal,
 "INTERMEDIATE," 12" long 12.50
"CMStP&P"—Cold steel chisel, 8" long 6.00
"CMStP&P RR"—Ball pein hammer, "FAIRMOUNT,"
 14" handle 6.50
"CMStP&P RR"—Track pick, "BEAVER FALLS,"
 36" handle 22.00
"CStPM&O RY"—Track adz, "BEAVER FALLS,"
 34" handle 22.50

"CStPM&O RY"—Single headed open ended curved wrench, 7" long 8.00
"CStPM&O RY"—Double headed open ended curved wrench, 13" long 12.00
"DSS&A RY"—Spiking maul, "SLUG DEVIL," 34½" handle 25.00
"GN"—Monkey wrench, all metal, size 12, "TRIMO," 11" long 10.00
"GN RY"—Hatchet, depot type, "TRUE TEMPER," 13½" handle 35.00
"GN RY"—Ball Pein hammer, "TRUE TEMPER," 16" handle 6.50
"GN RY"—Cold steel chisel, 7½" long 7.50
"GN RY CO."—Track shovel, "AMES HUSKEY," 38" long with handle 18.00
"IC"—Track adz, "ALDUSHT, CHGO.," 34" handle 10.00
"LS&MS"—Double headed open ended curved wrench, 12" long 15.00
"M&StL"—Hatchet, depot type, claw nail puller head, 15" handle 40.00

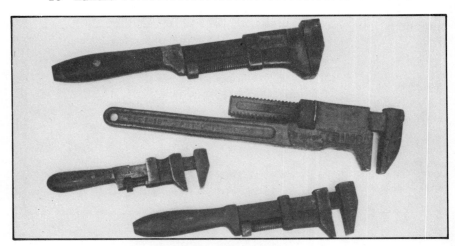

Various monkey wrenches

"M&StL"—Double faced sledge, 35" handle 15.00
"M&StL"—Cold steel chisel, 9" long 6.00
"NYC RR"—Cold steel chisel, 6½" long 4.00
"NYC&HR"—Double headed open ended curved wrench, 12" long 25.00
"NPR"—Monkey wrench, wood handle, "BILLINGS," 12½" long 12.50

"NPR"—Monkey wrench, wood handle, "B & Co.,"
15" long 12.00
"NPR"—Ball pein hammer, "TRUE TEMPER,"
16" handle 9.50
"NP RR"—Coal shovel, "AMES RED EDGE," 42½" long
with handle 20.00
"NP RR"—Hand saw, "E.C. ATKINS," wood handle, 26"
long 18.00
"NOR.PAC."—Steel chisel for gouging wood, 12½"
long 4.00
"OMAHA RY."—Monkey wrench, wood handle, "pat. 1901,
H.D. SMITH," 8½" long 15.00
"RY.EX.AGY."—Hatchet, depot type, "PLUMB," 14"
handle 35.00
"R.I. LINES"—Coal shovel, coal stove type, cast iron,
16½" long 25.00
"R.I. LINES"—Tie tongs, "ALDUSHT CO. CHGO."
29" long 26.00
"ROCK ISLAND"—Double headed open ended curved
wrench, 11½" long 10.00
"St.P.CY.RY."—Steel lining bar, 58½" long 16.00
" SOO LINE"—Spiking maul, "SLUG DEVIL," 34½"
handle 25.00
"SOO LINE"—Cold steel chisel, 8½" long 5.00
"UNION PACIFIC"—Monkey wrench, all metal,
"W&B RR SPECIAL," 8" long 11.00
"UNION PACIFIC"—Tool box, wood, iron handle,
28" long 11.00

TOURIST GUIDES AND BROCHURES

Railroad guidebooks were published as early as the 1850s. Many
were beautifully illustrated with colored maps, train schedules,
and interesting advertisements. Most of these were privately
published. Many of the early guidebooks have a very high value
placed on them. Those published by the railroads are especially
desirable.

Thousands of travel brochures were distributed by the railroads
down through the years encouraging the tourist to ride their

trains. Many were discarded after the trip ended, making them scarce today. Those from the early 1900s are the most colorful and interesting. Copies in fine condition bring good prices.

Among the numerous soft-cover books promoting tourist travel were the string-tied scenic guidebooks containing colored pictures of scenery along the railroad's route. These were in vogue in the early 1900s, and today collectors are seeking them out.

The railroads issued colorful brochures to lure the settlers, telling of the many farming advantages on the lands available along their right-of-way. Many collectors are interested in them.

GUIDE BOOKS

APPLETON'S—*Northern and Eastern Traveler's Guide,*
1853, hard cover 65.00
CROFUTT'S—*Trans-Continental Tourists' Guide,* 1871,
hard cover 50.00
HARPER'S—*New York and Erie Rail-Road Guide Book,*
1852, hard cover 75.00
HITTEL'S—*Hand Book of Pacific Coast Travel,* 1885,
hard cover 35.00
NELSON'S—*Pictorial Guide Book, Union Pacific
Railroad,* 1871, hard cover 30.00

String-tied scenic guide book

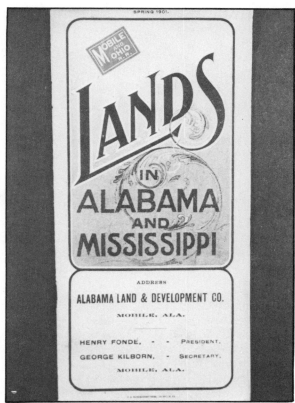

Settler's brochure

TRAVEL BROCHURES

C&NW—"Century of Progress," 1934, folder 3.50
D&H—"The Adirondacks, Our Great Natl. Playground,"
 folder, 1920s 7.50
D&RG—"Panoramic Views along the Scenic Line
 of the World," folder, 1893 . . . . .15.00
FEC—*East Coast of Florida,* booklet, 1900 . . . . .12.00

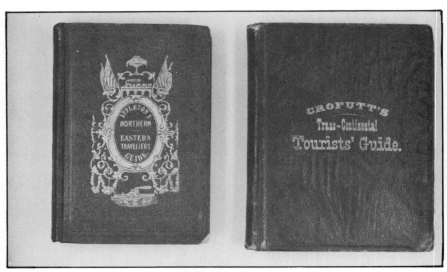

Early guide books

GN—*Seven Sunsets,* booklet, 1915 .10.00
GN—*The Oriental Limited,* booklet, 1914 . . . . .8.50
GN—"Glacier National Park, Hotels & Tours,"
 folder, 1915 . . . . .7.50
MIDLAND ROUTE—*Thru the Rockies of Colorado,*
 booklet, 1910 . . . . .18.00
LV—*In 3 States,* booklet, 1880s (rare) 35.00
NYC—"Hudson River, folder," 1934 . . . . .5.50
NP—*6000 Miles through Wonderland,* booklet,
 1893 . . . . .15.00
NP—*Along the Scenic Highway,* booklet, 1914 . . . . .12.50
PRR—"Eastern Tours Summer 1929," folder 4.50
ROCK ISLAND SYSTEM—"Across the Continent in a
 Tourist Sleeping Car," folder, 1903 . . . . .8.00
ROCK ISLAND—*California,* booklet, 1912 . . . . .8.00
SANTA FE—*The California Limited,* booklet,
 1914-1915 . . . . .7.50
SANTA FE—*Along Your Way,* booklet, 1949 . . . . .3.00
SOO LINE—*By Way of the Canyons,* booklet, 1907 . . . . . . .12.50

SOO LINE—"See Europe if You Will but see America
First," folder, 1907 ....10.00
SP&S—"The Scenic Columbia River," folder 7.50
UP—*A Glimpse of the Great Salt Lake*, booklet,
1894, (rare) 30.00
UP—*Summer Tours*, booklet, 1933 ....3.50

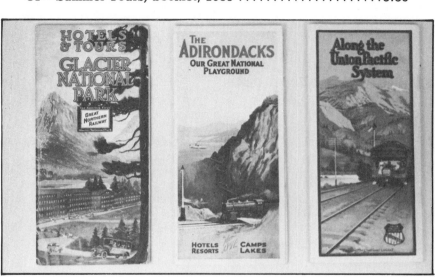

Tourist brochures

STRING-TIED SCENIC GUIDE BOOKS

CM&StP—*Lake Michigan to Puget Sound*,
1924 ....12.50
D&RG—*Rocky Mountain Views*, 1917 ....15.00
D&RG—*Heart of the Rockies*, 1910 ....20.00
M&PP—*The Pike's Peak Region*, 1922 ....12.50
SANTA FE—*The Great Southwest*, (Fred Harvey)
1914 ....35.00
SP—*The Shasta Route*, 1916 ....15.00
SP—*The Overland Trail*, 1923 ....12.50
WP—*From Salt Lake City to San Francisco Bay*,
1915 ....15.00

SETTLER'S ADVERTISING BROCHURES

CM&StP—"Three Forks Country, Montana," folder,
1913 ....7.50

TOY TRAINS

Collecting old toy trains is one of today's most popular hobbies, and an ever increasing number of railroadiana collectors are being attracted to them. Down through the years millions of these toy trains were made out of wood, tin, and cast iron, in pull type, friction, wind-up, live steam, and electric. Many collectors specialize in the cast-iron sets, while others collect the early wind-ups or electric models, but most generalize. Names most sought after are Ives, American Flyer, and Lionel. Condition is a very important factor in pricing. An early set in its original box in fine condition commands a very high price. Reproductions are being made.

Michigan Central cast iron set

WOOD—Pull type, set, locomotive/tender, two
passenger cars, lithographed designs on paper glued
to sides. ca. 1870 . . . . 300.00
TIN—Pull type, set, locomotive, 3 passenger cars, original
paint, length 22", ca. 1870s 200.00
CAST IRON—Pull type, set, locomotive, tender, two freight
cars, nickel finish, length 21", "pat. June 8, 1880,
Carpenter" 325.00

CAST IRON—4-4-0 type, locomotive with tender, original black finish, 21" long ca. 1880s. "Wilkins" 275.00

CAST IRON—set, #999 locomotive, tender, two cattle cars, original paint marked "M.C.R.R.," ca. 1890s 250.00

CAST IRON—#1101 locomotive, tender, two passenger cars, nickel finish, marked "C.R.I. & P.R.R.," ca. 1890s, "Wilkins" 325.00

CAST IRON—set, #857 locomotive, tender, four passenger cars, "Washington," "Narcissus," red/gold decor, "Pennsylvania R.R.Co. 1927, Hubley" 300.00

LIVE STEAM—set, locomotive, tender, baggage & two passenger cars, original paint, "VULCAN" Germany, ca. 1890s 500.00

WOOD/TIN—friction type, locomotive only, original red/gold trim decor, ca. 1900s 125.00

WIND-UP—"American Flyer," tinplate, O gauge set, locomotive, tender, three passenger cars, original box, ca. 1910 . . . . .200.00

WIND-UP—"Hafner's" tinplate, O gauge set, locomotive, tender, three passenger cars, "Overland Flyer," original red and yellow decor, ca. 1930s 125.00

ELECTRIC—Ives, O gauge set, electric type locomotive #3200, two passenger cars, litho "The Ives Railway Lines," ca. 1911 . . . . ・. 200.00

ELECTRIC—Ives, O gauge set, #1117 engine, tender, three passenger cars, litho "Limited Vestibule Express," ca. 1920s 275.00

ELECTRIC—Lionel, standard gauge set, #318E engine, three passenger cars, ca. 1930s 1,500.00

ELECTRIC—Lionel, O gauge set, #258 engine, tender, three passenger cars, original box, ca. 1930 . . . . .325.00

ELECTRIC—Lionel, O gauge set, #1666 engine, tender, gondola car, box car, milk car, caboose, original cartons, ca. 1950s 150.00

Vulcan, German live steam set

WATCHES, WATCH FOBS AND EMBLEM CHARMS

American watchmakers were required to meet certain rigid standards established by the railroads, including inspection and servicing routinely performed by qualified jewelers. It would be wise for the collector not knowledgeable of authentic railroad pocket watches to make a thorough study in this field before investing in them. The fact that a watch may have a train engraving on the case, for instance, does not necessarily mean that the movement is an approved railroad grade. Watches not in running order, or having dial cracks, or cases badly worn or dented, must be discounted. All watches listed here are in perfect condition.

Thousands of Brotherhood and railroad emblem charms were made to be worn on a gold watch chain across the vest. Also, fobs were made to be hung on a leather or woven wire mesh strap or black satin ribbon from the pant's watch pocket. These authentic old emblem charms and watch fobs are high on the list and command very good prices. There are current reproduction railroad watch fobs, leather strap type, on the market, and these should not be confused with the old.

Key to abbreviations
ADJ—movement has been adjusted to railroad specifications.
17J—number of jewels in the movement, 21J, 23J, etc.

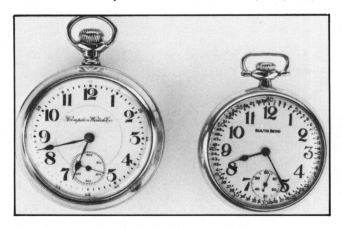

18 size and 16 size watches

5P—adjusted position of movement, as 5 positions, 6 positions, etc.

992—numbers denote model of movement and railroad grade.

16S—size of watch movement and case, 18 size large, 16 size smaller.

REG—regular standard arabic numeral dial.

MONT—Montgomery minute marginal numeral dial.

YGF—yellow gold filled case.

WGF—white gold filled case.

BALL—(Elgin) *333, 17J, 5P, 18S, REG*, silveroid case 275.00

BALL—(Hamilton) *17J, ADJ, 18S, REG*, silveroid case 200.00

BALL—(Hamilton) *999, 17J, 5P, 18S, REG*, silver case, train engraving 300.00

BALL—(Waltham) *17J, 5P, 16S, REG, YGF* case 180.00

BALL—(Illinois) *19J, 5P, 16S, REG, YGF* case 200.00

BALL—(Hamilton) *999, 21J, 5P, 18S*, sterling case, gold inlay locomotive 325.00

BALL—(Hamilton) *999B, 21J, 6P, 16S, MONT, YGF* case 325.00

BALL—(Hamilton) *21J, 5P, 16S, REG, WGF* case 245.00

BALL—(Hamilton) *23J, 5P, 16S, REG, YGF* case 600.00

BALL—(Swiss) *21J, 6P, 16S, REG, YGF* case 275.00

ELGIN—*17J, ADJ, 18S*, key wind, Roman numeral dial, *YGF* hunting case, locomotive engraving 165.00

ELGIN—B.W. RAYMOND, *19J, 5P, 18S*, up & down indicator dial, *YGF* case 750.00

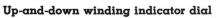

Up-and-down winding indicator dial

ELGIN—B.W. RAYMOND, *21J, 5P, 16S, REG, YGF*
case 175.00
ELGIN—Father Time, *21J, 5P, 16S, MONT, YGF*
case 165.00
ELGIN—*379, 21J, 5P, 18S, REG, YGF* case 160.00
ELGIN—Veritas, *21J, 5P, 16S, REG, YGF* case 185.00
ELGIN—Veritas, *23J, ADJ, 18S, REG, YGF* case locomotive
engraving 285.00
ELGIN—Veritas, *23J, 5P, 18S, REG, YGF* case 325.00
HAMILTON—*17J, ADJ, 18S,* Roman numeral dial, *YGF*
hunting case, train engraving 200.00
HAMILTON—*996, 19J, 5P, 16S, REG, YGF* case 275.00
HAMILTON—*940, 21J, 5P, 18S, MONT, YGF* case 150.00
HAMILTON—*992, 21J, 5P, 16S, MONT, YGF* case 150.00
HAMILTON—*992B, 21J, 6P, 16S, REG, YGF* case 200.00
HAMILTON—*950, 23J, 5P, 16S,* dial marked "23 Jewels-
Railway Special," *YGF* case 425.00
HAMILTON—*950B, 23J, 6P, 16S,* dial marked "23 Jewels-
Railway Special," *YGF* case 450.00
HAMPDEN—*17J,* Special Adjusted, *18S,* Roman numeral
dial, *YGF* hunting case, locomotive engraving 225.00
HAMPDEN—New Railway, *21J, 5P, REG, WGF* case 175.00
HAMPDEN—Railway Special, *21J, ADJ, 18S, REG,* sterling
case, gold inlay locomotive 195.00
HAMPDEN—Special Railway, *21J, 5P, 18S, REG, YGF*
case 225.00
HAMPDEN—Special Railway, *23J, 5P, 18S, REG, YGF*
case 350.00
HOWARD—Railroad Chronometer Series *10, 21J, 5P, 16S,*
REG, YGF case 275.00

Brotherhood and railroad emblem charms

HOWARD—Railroad Chronometer Series *11*, *21J*, *5P*, *16S*,
  MONT, *YGF* case 285.00
ILLINOIS—Abe Lincoln, *21J*, *5P*, *16S*, Ferguson dial,
  YGF case 275.00
ILLINOIS—Bunn Special, *21J*, *6P*, *16S*, *REG*, *YGF*
  case, locomotive engraving 185.00
ILLINOIS—Bunn Special, 60 Hour, *21J*, *6P*, *16S*, *REG*,
  YGF case 275.00
ILLINOIS—Burlington Special, *21J*, *ADJ*, *16S*, *MONT*,
  YGF case 185.00
ILLINOIS—Sangamo Special, *21J*, *6P*, *16S*, *REG*, *YGF*
  case 225.00
ILLINOIS—Sangamo Special, *23J*, *6P*, *16S*, *MONT*,
  YFG case 395.00
ILLINOIS—Santa Fe Special, *21J*, *ADJ*, *16S*, *MONT*,
  YGF case, train engraving 195.00
ROCKFORD—*545*, *21J*, *5P*, *16S*, *REG*, *YGF* case 150.00
ROCKFORD—*505*, *21J*, *5P*, *16S*, *REG*, *YGF* case 150.00
ROCKFORD—*918*, *21J*, *5P*, *18S*, *MONT*, sterling case,
  locomotive engraving 200.00
SOUTH BEND—*227*, *21J*, *5P*, *16S*, *MONT*, *YGF* case 150.00
SOUTH BEND—Studebaker, *21J*, *8P*, *16S REG*, *WGF*
  case 185.00
SOUTH BEND—*295*, *21J*, *5P*, *16S*, *MONT*, *YGF*
  case 175.00
WALTHAM—Riverside, *19J*, *5P*, *16S*, *MONT*, *YGF*
  case 195.00

**Strap, wire mesh, and
black satin ribbon fobs**

WALTHAM—Vanguard, *19J, 5P, 16S,* Canadian dial,
   YGF case 185.00
WALTHAM—Crescent Street, *21J, 5P, 16S, MONT, YGF*
   case 195.00
WALTHAM—*645, 21J, 5P, 16S, REG, YGF* case 275.00
WALTHAM—*845, 21J, 5P, 18S, REG, YGF* case 125.00
WALTHAM—Vanguard, *21J, ADJ, 18S,* Canadian dial,
   silveroid case, locomotive engraving 155.00
WALTHAM—Maximum, *23J, ADJ, 16S, REG,* 18K gold
   case 750.00
WALTHAM—Vanguard, *23J, 6P, 16S, REG, YGF*
   case 275.00
WALTHAM—Vanguard, *23J, 6P, 16S,* Up & Down
   indicator dial, *YGF,* case 495.00

WATCH FOBS AND EMBLEM CHARMS

"DAVENPORT LOCOMOTIVE WORKS, DAVENPORT
   IOWA"—Oval, silver plated copper, locomotive in
   center, leather strap type 85.00
"INT'L. ASSN. OF RWY. SPECIAL AGENTS AND
   POLICE"—round, bronze, train encricled by "Safety First"
   on blue enamel, leather strap type 65.00
"RAILWAY SIGNAL ASSOCIATION"—round, brass, train
   and semaphores in center, leather strap type 55.00
"STANLEY MERRILL & PHILLIPS RY. CO., STANLEY,
   WISC."—oval, bronze, locomotive center, "1909" above,
   "Spur 5" below, leather strap type 75.00
"LADIES AUXILLARY O.R.C. MEMPHIS 1907"—ornate
   bronze fob, leather strap type 55.00
"NORTHERN PACIFIC"—monad logo, enamel on gold,
   black satin ribbon type 85.00
"ASSOC. SOCIETY OF LOCOMOTIVE ENGINEERS &
   FIREMAN"—ornate gold/enamel emblem, black satin
   ribbon type 95.00
"BROTHERHOOD OF RAILWAY TRAINMEN"—ornate gold/
   enamel BRT emblem, woven wire mesh type 45.00
"BROTHERHOOD OF LOCOMOTIVE FIREMEN AND
   ENGINEERS"—ornate gold/enamel emblem, vest
   chain type 35.00
"BROTHERHOOD OF RAILROAD TRAINMEN"—maltese
   cross type, gold/black enamel, BRT insignia at center,
   vest chain emblem charm 35.00
"KANSAS CITY SOUTHERN"—bronze disc 1" diameter,
   Golden Spike Anniversary, 1897-1947," vest chain
   fob 15.00

"NORTHERN PACIFIC"—inlay enamel monad logo on gold filled disc, 1 1/8" diameter, vest chain emblem charm 25.00

WAX SEALERS AND ACCESSORIES

These are small hand tools used by railroad Station Agents to safeguard envelopes and packages containing currency or valuable items with wax seals. They were made with either a fancy or plain wood handle attached to a bronze or brass matrix, or they came entirely in one-piece brass or bronze. The matrix had indented letters and numbers stamped in reverse, producing a legible impression in the wax seal. Wax sealers were discontinued shorty after World War II. Those from early, now defunct roads have a higher value. All wax sealers listed here are in perfect condition, with their original handles. Those with the matrix badly scratched, nicked, or defaced, or with cracked, chipped, or replaced handles, are discounted in price.

Express companies also used wax sealers, and these parallel those of the railroads and are also being collected. Wells Fargo Express appears to be the most popular and brings the higher prices in this group. Wax sealers that are dual marked, with both

Railroad and express company wax sealers

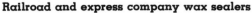

railroad and express company names, are rarities and command top prices.

The various torches, lamps, and other implements used in melting the sealing wax, including the sticks of sealing wax, the early money package envelopes forwarded by railroads and express companies, are also being picked up as accessories to the wax sealers. They bring good prices, too.

RAILROAD

"AT&SF RY—Agent, Gage, Okla.," tall iron
handle 95.00
"AT&SF RY—Agent, Lyons, Kans.," brass toadstool
handle 75.00
"B&ME RR—Agent, Charlestown, N.H.," wood
handle 75.00
"B&MR RR CO—No. 59," fancy wood handle 150.00
"B&MR RR—In Neb., Nelson," brass toadstool
handle 150.00
"CB&Q RR CO—Randolph, Ia.," hollow brass
handle 75.00
"CB&Q RR—Bussey, Iowa," fancy wood handle 95.00

"C&EI RR—Fountain Creek, Ill.," wood handle 65.00
"C&G RY. CO—Agent, Elizabeth, Miss.," wood
handle 75.00
"CGW RR—142, New Hampton, Ia.," hollow brass
handle 125.00
"CGW RR—Forest Park, Ill.," wood handle 95.00

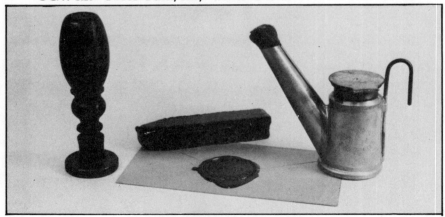

Utensil for melting sealing wax

"CM&StP RY—F.S. Div. Fargo," brass toadstool
handle 75.00
"CM&StP RY—Mitchell Station," wood handle 75.00
"CM&StP RY. CO—S.M. Div. Fedora," wood
handle 75.00
"CM&StP RY. CO—S.C. & D. Div. Stickney," wood
handle 75.00
"CMStP&P RR CO—S.M. Div. Madison, S.Dk.,"
wood handle 75.00
"CRI&P RY—Agent, Banks, Ar.," hollow brass
handle 75.00
"CRI&P RY—Agent, Hope, Minn.," wood handle 65.00
"C&NW RY—Station, Faulkton," brass toadstool
handle 85.00
"C&NW RY—Agent, Geneva, Neb.," hollow brass
handle 75.00
"CStPM&O RY CO—Herman, Neb.," brass toadstool
handle 100.00
"GC&SF RY—Ballinger, Tex.," brass toadstool
handle 75.00
"GF&A RY—Agent, Local, Ala.," brass toadstool
handle 85.00
"GN RY CO—A-13 Dining Car Dept.," wood handle 75.00
"GREAT NORTHERN RY. CO—Anoka, Minn.," brass
toadstool handle 85.00
"GTR—Groveton," brass toadstool handle 75.00
"IC RR CO—Leroy, Ill.," brass toadstool handle 100.00
"IC RR—Agent, Barnes," fancy wood handle 85.00
"IC RR—Ticket Office, Hills, Minn.," hollow brass
handle 75.00
"ILL. SO. RY—Agent, Flat River, Mo.," brass toadstool
handle 95.00
"KCM&B RR—Sullicent, Alabama," iron bulb
handle 115.00
"KCStJ&CB RR—Amazonia, Mo.," hollow brass
handle 165.00
"KANSAS CITY SOUTHERN RY—Freight Station, Joplin,"
wood handle 95.00
"L&N RR CO—Agent, K.C. 190, Paris, Ky.," wood
handle 75.00
"M-K-T RR CO—Agent, Deefield, Mo.," brass
toadstool handle 75.00
"M&NW RR CO—New Hampton, Ia.," brass toadstool
handle 175.00
"M&O RR" Brass toadstool handle 75.00
"M&StP RY—Algona," wood toadstool handle 175.00

"MO PAC RY CO—Agent, Chatfield, Ark.," brass
toadstool handle 75.00
"MO PAC RY CO—168," iron bulb handle 75.00
"NEW YORK CENTRAL RR—B 184; Albany, N.Y.," wood
handle 75.00
"NOR PAC RY CO—Maddock, N.D.," brass toadstool
handle 85.00
"NOR PAC RR—Anoka," brass toadstool handle 85.00
"NWP RR—Willits," wood handle 75.00
"PW&B RR CO—212," pewter toadstool handle 95.00
"RRI&StL RR—Bushnell," wood handle 165.00
"SC RR CO—29, Agency," wood bulb handle 100.00
"SOUTHERN RY CO—Branchville, S.C.," wood bulb
handle 75.00
"SOU PAC CO—Marshfield, Ore.," wood bulb
handle 75.00
"TStL&KC RR—144," fancy wood handle 150.00
"UNION PACIFIC—548," wood handle 75.00
"WABASH RR CO—37," nickel toadstool handle 85.00
"WABASH RR—Dining Car Dept.," nickel toadstool
handle 125.00
"WP RR CO—Agent, Westwood," wood handle 75.00
"WC RR—Ore Docks, Ashland, Wis.," fancy wood
handle 135.00
"WIS CEN LINES—Ironwood, Mich.," wood handle 125.00
"WStL&P RY—No. 197, Dining Car," brass toadstool
handle 150.00
"W&StP RR—Redwood Falls Station," hollow brass
handle 150.00

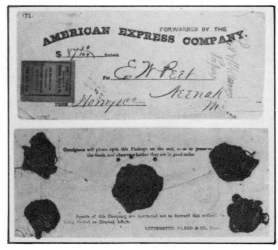

**Early express cover
with wax seals intact**

"Y&MV RR CO—Isola, Miss.," brass toadstool
handle 95.00

RAILROAD AND EXPRESS DUAL MARKED

"AM. RY. EX. CO., C&NW—Merrill, Iowa,"
wood handle 175.00
"NAT'L. EX. CO., NO. 7, C&A RR" wood handle 200.00
"NOR.PAC.EXP., NP RR CO—Clear Lake, Minn.,"
hollow brass handle 250.00
"RY.EX.AGY. INC., CGW—Clarkesville, Iowa," wood
handle 185.00

EXPRESS COMPANY

"ADAMS EXPRESS COMPANY—5186, Burlington, Iowa,"
broad toadstool handle 85.00
"AM. EX. CO.—No. 2, Atalissa, Iowa," iron bulb
handle 75.00
"AMERICAN EXPRESS CO—Milroy, Minn.," nickel bulb
handle 45.00
"AMERICAN RAILWAY EXPRESS CO—Fingal, N.D.,"
hollow brass handle 27.50
"AMERICAN RAILWAY EXPRESS CO—2154, Messenger,"
wood handle 25.00
"CANADIAN PACIFIC EXPRESS—653," brass toadstool
handle 125.00
"NATIONAL EXP.CO—Willshire, Ohio," wood bulb
handle 95.00
"NOR. PAC. EX. CO—746, Goven, Wash.," brass
toadstool handle 175.00
"RY.EX.AGY.INC—Public, Hastings, Minn.," wood
handle 27.50
"RY.EX.AGY. INC—Shelton, Neb.," hollow brass
handle 30.00
"SOUTHERN EXPRESS COMPANY—534" wood bulb
handle 35.00
"SOUTHERN EX. CO.—4797 Whitakers, N.C." brass
toadstool handle 42.50
"WELLS FARGO & CO.'S EXPRESS—Hampton, Minn.,"
wood bulb handle 150.00
"WELLS FARGO & CO. EXPRESS—442," iron bulb
handle 100.00
"WELLS FARGO & CO. EXPRESS—Southard, Okla.,"
hollow brass handle 125.00

WAX SEALING ACCESSORIES

SEALING WAX—stick, railroad marked, old stock,
    used 1.00
SEALING WAX—box, railroad marked, new stock, brown,
    four sticks, 5/8" square, 10½" long 5.00
SEALING WAX—box, Express marked, new stock, red,
    four sticks, 5/8" square, 10½" long 5.00
UTENSIL—for melting sealing wax, torch type, height
    2½", tin, spout with wick, hook handle 35.00
UTENSIL—for melting sealing wax, lamp type, height
    2½", brass, enameled, cap for wick, regular
    handle 65.00
UTENSIL—for melting sealing wax, tray type, 3½" x 5½",
    brass, complete with alcohol burner and ladle 85.00
MONEY PACKAGE ENVELOPE—Express Co., early,
    original wax seal impressions on backside
    (scarce) 25.00
MONEY PACKAGE ENVELOPE—Railroad, early, original
    wax seal impressions on backside (scarce) 35.00
MONEY PACKAGE ENVELOPE—Railroad, pre-WW II,
    unused 5.00
MONEY PACKAGE ENVELOPE—Rwy. Ex. Agency, 1950s,
    unused 3.50

WOOD TOKENS

Wood tokens were made of brass or copper, varying in size from
a nickel to a half-dollar. They had the denominations of ¼ to 1
cord wood stamped on them, along with the engine number.
Some also had the railroad's initials included on them. In the
early days of wood-burning locomotives, these were used by the
railroads in payment for cord wood supplied by farmers and
others at fueling stops along the railroad's right-of-way. The
railroad had money in the home office or on deposit in various
banks where they could be redeemed. These tokens are very
scarce and carry a premium price.

"M.C.R.R. 112"—stamped on obverse, "½ cord" on
    reverse, brass 85.00
"M.C.R.R."—stamped on obverse, "½ cord Eng. 13"
    on reverse, brass 85.00

192

Brass cord wood token

"M.S. & N.I.R.R. - E & N Div."—raised on obverse,
  "¼ cord, Eng. 48" on reverse, copper 95.00
"WOOD—Engine No. 136, ½ cord"—stamped on obverse,
  reverse blank, brass 75.00

MISCELLANEOUS THINGS

There will always be miscellaneous things and odds and ends
turning up. The question is, "What price will they bring?" Here
are a number of them not included in the foregoing categories.

BELL—horse, early street railway, cast brass, raised
  letters "ST. P. CITY RY. CO." around bottom skirt,
  3" high, 3" diameter, original iron clapper 150.00
BRAKEMAN'S CLUB—wood, 28" long, marked
  "M&StL RY CO. Hartwell Hickory trademark" 20.00
BROOM—depot, handle length 38" with 16" straws,
  railroad marked, "made by O.K.Broom Co., Chgo." ...10.00
BROOM—track, handle length 33" with 8" metal
  tip, 14" heavy duty straws "OK Broom Co., Chgo." 12.50
BRUSH—coach seats, "N.Y.C.&H.R. R.R." early
  1900s 17.00

Police whistles

Bulletin board

BULLETIN BOARD—depot, train arrival and departures, wood, black, 30" x 36". UP shield logos and name across top 95.00

COAT HANGER—wood, marked "THE PROPERTY OF THE PULLMAN CO." 8.00

DEPOT CLOCK—Seth Thomas, wall, eight-day, marked "SOO LINE" 225.00

DINING CAR CHIMES—with mallet, "Deagan, Chgo." 45.00

DOOR PLATE—depot, brass, cast SOO LINE logo above doorknob hole, 3½" x 16½" 35.00

FEATHER DUSTER—coach, wood handle with turkey feathers, 24" long, railroad marked 25.00

FIRE EXTINGUISHER—brass, Pyrene, 14" tall with wall mount back panel and locking strap, railroad marked 35.00

FIRE EXTINGUISHER—glass tube, chemical type, 18" long, embossed "C&NW RY.," cast iron wall brackets 65.00

FLASHLIGHT—Bakelite, two cells, 7" long, incised "AT&SF RY CO." 12.50

LAMPSHADE—ceiling, depot, metal, green enameled outside, white inside, 14" diameter 12.50

LAMP—depot platform, pole mounted, kerosene, burns
24 hours, adjustable self-extinguishing device, "Dietz,"
early 1900s 300.00
LEAD SEAL PRESS—"RAILWAY EXPRESS AGENCY,"
cast iron, shaped like pliers, 10" long, imprints
number and location on lead disc, used for sealing
cloth bags 35.00
PAINT BRUSH—pure bristle, 2" long, "PRR" monogram on
handle, "Rubico" 8.00
POKER CHIPS—set of 60 in box, 20 each, blue, red,
white, both sides marked with G.N. RY. goat
logo 50.00
POLICE WHISTLE—brass, "B&O RR" incised on
top 25.00
POLICE WHISTLE—black plastic, "PRR" monogram
inlaid at side 15.00
RAILROAD SPIKE—narrow gauge road, "Colorado,"
4½" long 1.00
RAILROAD SPIKE—standard gauge, 6" long, gold plated,
souvenir of steam excursion trip, railroad marked 5.00
SCALE—counter type, two-sided dial, weighs up to
60 lbs., pan marked "RY. EX. AGY.," cast iron base,
6" wide, 17" long 125.00
SEMAPHORE SIGNAL ARM—metal, original paint, three
colored glass lenses, red, yellow and green,
72" long 75.00
STEEL RAIL—narrow gauge road, "Colorado," cut and
polished desk piece, 3" high, 3" long, dated
1882 . . . . .8.00

Stoneware jugs

STONEWARE JUG—10¼" high, 7" diameter, top part brown, "ROCK ISLAND LINES" in blue stenciled on white under glaze in front 75.00

STONEWARE JUG—11" high, 7" diameter, top part brown, "CHICAGO, ST. PAUL, MINNEAPOLIS AND OMAHA RAILWAY CO." stenciled in blue on front. "Stop Look Now Listen Coal Waste And Oil cost money Let's save it on this run Please"—stenciled on backside 100.00

Railway express counter scale

STONEWARE JUG—9" high, 5½" dia., top part brown, "DEODORIZER, THE PULLMAN COMPANY" stenciled in blue around front on light grey 50.00

STRONG BOX—metal, key locked, hinged lid, 13½" x 20" x 11", original paint, lettered "D.S.S. & A. RY." across front 150.00

TETHER WEIGHT—cast iron, 8" diameter, 2½" high, 30 lbs., raised letters around top, "AM. RY. EX. CO." with serial number 150.00

THERMOMETER—wall, metal, 2½" x 10", "G.N. RY." with indented black numerals on brass background, "Taylor" 50.00

TIMETABLE HOLDER—wall type, metal, 8¾" x 12" x 4" deep, for depot use, railroad marked in front 65.00

TRAIN ORDER—CGW, 1965 .... 1.00

TRAIN ORDER HOOP—bentwood type, with metal clip attachment to hold train orders, length, 48" 37.50

TRAIN ORDER HOOP—wood/metal, "Y" shape, Hi-Speed Delivery type, train orders string-tied. Length, 70" 25.00

WASTE BASKET—wire grill type, tin pie-plate bottom, 14" tall 15.00

RAILROAD-RELATED COLLECTIBLES

There are objects in the form of the locomotive and many items picturing the train to be found. Although these are not authentic railroadiana items, those who generalize will usually include some of them in their collection. Here is a representative listing.

BANK—locomotive, pot metal, bronze finish, "Railroadman's Federal," ca. 1920s 25.00

BIRTHDAY CAKE TRAIN—ceramic, 6 pieces, locomotive, circus cars and caboose 15.00

BOTTLE—snuff, dark amber, 4½" tall, "Railroad Mills," train on label 30.00

BREAD PLATTER—clear glass, 9" x 12", Fast Mail Train" impressed, ca. 1880s 75.00

CALENDAR—Traveler's Insurance, 1885, engraving of train 75.00

CANDY CONTAINER—locomotive, glass with lithographed tin closure depicting cab interior 25.00

CANDY CONTAINER—locomotive, glass, "999," tin screw cap closure rear 45.00

CANDY CONTAINER—railroad lantern, red glass, tin flared base and top, wire handle, 3¾" high 15.00

Early
chewing tobacco tin

CANDY CONTAINER—signal lantern, green glass,
tin screw top closure, wire handle, 3½" high 12.50
CHOCOLATE MOLD—early 6-wheel locomotive, tin,
5" x 6" 65.00
CIGAR BOX—"Soo Line," steam train on cover, early
1900s 25.00
CRACKER JACK PRIZE—tin locomotive "No. 512,"
ca. 1920s 10.00
CRAYONS—"Dixon Railroad," white chalk crayon
for marking freight cars, etc., 4" long sticks, box,
one gross 10.00
CUP & SAUCER—old time locomotive and coaches,
"England," ca. 1930s 25.00
DOMINOES—box, "Double Nine," train on cover, engine
embossed on dominoes, ca. 1910 . . . . 35.00
FLASK—"Lowell Railroad," amber, ½ pint, early
19th century 200.00
FLASK—"Success To The Railroad," olive green, pint,
early 19th century 180.00
GREETING POSTCARD—birthday, toy locomotive,
Germany, 1910 . . . . 7.50
MAGIC LANTERN—glass slide picturing train,
Germany 5.00
MATCH SAFE—pewter, early locomotive, embossed
both sides 50.00
MIRROR—pocket, advertising, "Traveler's Ins. Co.,"
picture of passenger train at night 35.00

Tin railroad heralds, cereal premiums — 1950s

Old glass candy containers

MUG—china, old-time locomotive and coaches, "B & T" hallmark, England, ca. 1890s 65.00

PAPERWEIGHT—medallion type, 3" diameter, bronze, advertising item, "The National Lock Washer Co., Newark, N.J.," passenger train depicted in center, ca. 1920s 35.00

PINBACK—celluloid, 1" diameter, advertising, "Metro-Goldwyn Pictures," steam train pictured in center, ca. 1930s 5.00

PLATE—china, "Currier & Ives Express Train, Adams," ca. 1930s 75.00

POCKET KNIFE—photo of mallet locomotive, 4¼" long, ca. 1910 ....50.00

Occupational shaving mug

POCKET KNIFE—"Traveler's Ins. Co.," embossed steam
train, 3¼" long, ca. 1910 ....35.00
POCKET WATCH—Ingram $1.00 watch, kids, locomotive
on dial and back cover, ca. 1930s 35.00
POSTER—Circus, "Ringling Bros. Barnum & Bailey,"
railroad scene, 26" x 39" 150.00
RAILROAD HERALDS—tin, set of 28, cereal premiums,
1950s 50.00
RAILROAD HERALDS—tin, set of 25 only, three missing
from original set, re-runs, late 1970s 15.00
SHAVING BRUSH—old time locomotive, England,
recent 10.00
SHAVING MUG—Occupational, locomotive, ca.
1875 ....125.00
SHAVING MUG—Occupational, baggage car, ca.
1910 ....100.00
SHAVING MUG—old time locomotive, England,
recent 15.00
SIGN—tin, advertising, "Pay Car Chewing Tobacco,"
railroad pay car 50.00
SIGN—tin, advertising, "Altoona Beers," horseshoe curve
and trains, 1950s 75.00
SPOON—souvenir, sterling, "Altoona, Pa.," train on
handle, horseshoe curve in bowl, dated 1906 ....18.00
STEIN—porcelain, lithopane base, "Corps. of Ry. Const.
Engineers," locomotive on pewter lid, Germany,
1884 ....150.00
STEVENSGRAPH—Train, "The Present Time," Great
Britain 75.00
STICKPIN—"Travelers Ins. Co., Hartford, Conn." raised
locomotive on small gold plated disc, early
1900s 25.00
TOOTSIETOY—Pennsylvania locomotive 4-6-2 type,
6" long, pot metal 15.00
TRADECARD—Soapine, model locomotive, ca.
1880s 4.00
TRINKET BOX—locomotive, Staffordshire, ca.
1890s 55.00
TOBACCO TIN—Fast Mail Train on cover, pat.
1878 ....150.00
POSTER—motion picture, "Rock Island Trail,"
ca. 1950s 25.00
POSTAGE STAMP—U.S. 1901, Pan American issue,
2¢, passenger train, unused, very fine 40.00
POSTAGE STAMP—U.S. 1912, Parcel Post issue, 5¢,
mail train, unused, very fine 30.00